TRUSTING

TRUSTING

The issue at the heart of every relationship

by

Pat Springle

Highland Books

Originally published in the United States of America by Vine Books.

First published in England in 1995 by Highland Books, Two High Pines, Knoll Road, Godalming, Surrey GU7 2EP

Library Cataloguing-in-Publication Data. A catalogue record for this book is available from the British Library.

Cover Design: Sally Maltby

ISBN: 1 897913 12 5

Printed in Great Britain by HarperCollins, Glasgow

Contents

ACKNOWLEDGMENTS

MANY PEOPLE have played significant roles in the creation of this book.

- For the umpteenth time, Sandy Ballard deciphered my many legal pads of chicken-scratch and turned them into legible words.

- Lee Carter and Stuart Rothberg gave me valuable insights and feedback on the manuscript. Also, Lee created the assessment checklists for the three types of mistrust.

- The people in our group at church provided the real stimulus for this book. Their questions and perspectives sharpened my thoughts about trust and mistrust.

- The people at Servant Publications, Don Cooper, Ann Spangler, Liz Heaney, and Beth Feia have been both partners and friends in this process.

- Pam Moran rearranged and edited the book to make it clearer.

- My family, Joyce, Catherine, and Taylor, continue to walk with me in the real-life, up-and-down path of learning to trust.

PART ONE

✦ ✦ ✦

What Is Trust?

1

Intangible Glue

WHOM DO YOU TRUST?
This question elicits a wide variety of responses. One woman remarked, "My husband gets absorbed in his work sometimes and forgets to let me know he'll be late for supper, but I know I can count on him when I really need him. He gets preoccupied sometimes, but that's okay. He's committed to me and the children."

Others mention special friends who always seem willing to listen and guard confidences, a wife who cares more about the family than climbing the social ladder, or an approachable pastor who doesn't feel compelled to be "the answer man" with all the right responses.

You may be trusting an impersonal company for a regular paycheck, the police department for adequate protection, a friend not to gossip about you, the Lord to forgive you for being selfish, or a spouse not to make fun of your broadening girth or the vanishing forest on the top of your head.

Trust is earned by consistently listening, giving, forgiving, and acting. How much could you trust an employer who forgot to issue your paycheck every so often? How much could you trust a friend who listens to your secrets but occasionally spreads gossip about you? Would you trust a spouse who had had an affair only two or three times? How much trust would you place in a parent who abruptly explodes in anger at your mistakes?

We can't expect perfection in the daily interactions of life, of course. We can put up with someone who usually listens to us but occasionally lapses into oblivion behind a newspaper or mumbles instant answers to get us out of the way—especially if they apologize for their inattention to our needs. But in order to build any sense of security and expectation of having our hopes fulfilled, we all need consistency.

Whether in family life or in the business world or in a sports arena—and especially in clutch situations—consistency overshadows occasional brilliance. A basketball commentator like Billy Packer may tell the fans, "The Tar Heels will try to get the ball to Williams for the last shot. He's their most consistent shooter."

I remember a particularly poignant scene in the movie *Hoosiers*, based on a true story. Having fought its way through the regular season and survived the play-offs, the basketball team from a small, rural high school now found itself in the state championship game. Second half. Only seconds to play. The star of the big-city favorite sank a shot to go up by one. The gutsy coach of the underdog Hoosiers used a time-out to call a surprise play: "They'll be looking for Jimmy, so let's fake to him and pass to Bill at the top of the key."

When the boys all looked disappointed and disgusted, the coach yelled, "What's the matter with you guys?"

Every eye turned to the quiet but confident young man whose golden jump shot had brought them to the brink of an incredible state championship. "I can make the shot," Jimmy said softly.

After a second's hesitation, the coach changed the play. "OK then, pass the ball to Jimmy at the top of the key."

The referee handed the ball to the player out of bounds. A quick pass to Jimmy. The twenty-foot jump shot at the buzzer … swish! The little team from the country had beaten the best in the state on a shot by their most consistent player.

The players trusted Jimmy so much that their nonverbal messages came through loud and clear. The coach trusted the players enough to receive their input and alter his game plan. And Jimmy trusted in his God-given talents enough to make the most important shot of his life. The opportunity for glory knocked on this young man's door and found him trustworthy.

A TWO-WAY STREET

Trust is central to our relationship with God, but Scripture makes no attempt to define it. The biblical writers are content to describe and illustrate in scores of ways how this intangible glue cements our relationships with God and other people. We use words such as "faith" and "belief" as synonyms for trust, but other words such as "hope" closely parallel and enhance our understanding.

Today, we use the word "hope" to mean "wish," such as "I hope it doesn't rain this weekend. We plan to go to the beach." But hope originally carried with it a sense of expectancy and anticipation. In Psalm 130, the writer encouraged believers to hope in the Lord:

O Israel, hope in the Lord;
For with the Lord there is lovingkindness,
And with him is abundant redemption. **Psalm 130:7**

Their hope was based on the character of God: his kindness, love, and forgiveness. But they were not to "wish" that God would come through; they could be certain. In a poetic and graphic metaphor, the psalmist was as sure of God's faithfulness as the guard in the watchtower was sure of the sun rising (Ps 130:6).

Human beings, however, are not nearly so faithful. How do we decide whether or not to place our trust in a particular person? We base our decision on two types of input: our perception of that person's character, and our own willingness to take appropriate risks. Many possible variables can ensue from this interpersonal dynamic. We may trust someone who soon proves untrustworthy. We often fail to trust those who are eminently trustworthy (God, for instance). Most human beings turn out to be trustworthy in some ways but not in others. And the ease with which we feel able to trust anyone can ebb and flow rather unpredictably.

Trust should not be universally granted. It is foolish to trust someone who has never been trustworthy in the past. Similarly, we need to be cautious about risking our vulnerability, our reputation, our time, and our money with someone we don't know well. Prudence dictates that we withhold trust until someone's character has been proven to warrant our confidence—and that we grant trust only to the degree to which it does so.

Our lives encompass a complex matrix of relationships—family, work, church, neighbors, and friends—which includes all ages and all points on the pecking order of authority. Every relationship remains quite fluid. The reliability of someone can unexpectedly change, perhaps due to an overload of stress or a financial collapse.

Our own ability to accurately perceive a person's trustworthiness can also change, either due to similar causes or for no apparent reason at all. Our ability to take risks can be diminished by fear or foolishness. Faltering communications quickly deprive a relationship's engine of both the oil which lubricates the working parts as well as the gas which provides energy.

Trust is based on feeling safe and secure, even in the face of real or perceived perils. Like multiple safety nets beneath a high-wire circus act, our sense of security can stem from many sources: a stable job, a substantial savings account, good health, a supportive marriage, friends, and a close-knit family, for example. Whether a relationship involves an employer, a banker, a doctor, a spouse, a neighbor, or a brother, we must learn who is trustworthy and who is not. We learn how much we can trust certain people and what limits exist to their trustworthiness. We gradually develop both our own perception about others, as well as our own capacity to trust.

Relationships which provide safety and promote trust are based on mutual esteem. Respect, dignity, and integrity work both ways, even when one person is much younger or when a parent provides care for a child. While the father or mother may demand respect in the form of obedience, he or she should also communicate respect by taking time to listen, to play, and to be interested in the child's efforts.

Similarly, respect for a spouse's feelings sends a helpful message: "I may not understand why you feel that way, but I care about you. I won't try to fix you or correct you. I value you as you are." When we condemn others for their emotions, or try to control how they act, or withdraw from them, we fail to communicate personal regard.

We may try to express how much we value others by fixing their problems, but these rescue attempts are often designed to make *us* feel better. One woman told her husband how to talk, how to eat, what to wear, what books to read, how to do his job—virtually everything except how to breathe (and she seemed poised on the brink for that one, too!). When a friend pointed out how her behavior robbed her husband of his self-confidence, she said disgustedly, "I'm only doing it for his own good."

THE STING OF DISAPPOINTMENT

All of us have felt the sting of trusting someone and being disappointed. The intensity of our hurt reflects the depth of our expectations. On one end of the wide continuum, a nearby stranger may passively watch while you struggle with luggage or packages or small children. This man could have offered to help but he didn't. Your expectations may have been so low that you didn't even notice his lack of willingness.

Farther up the scale, your boss may lavish praise on a fellow employee, even though *you* did most of the work on the project. Closer to home, a special friend fails to call on your birthday. You wonder what could account for this lapse in memory. Was it something you did?

Disappointments can devastate us regardless of age or lifestyle. A seven-year-old girl may feel crushed when her grandmother fails to come for an expected visit. A high school student may jump through all the hoops by wearing the right clothes, saying the right things, and hanging out with the right people, but still be rejected by his peer group. A single, forty-three-year-old woman may desperately hope the next man will treat her better. Or maybe the next one, or the next.... After twenty-eight years of marriage, a husband may make some snickering remarks about his wife's weight. The fact that he has lost interest in her sexually rubs salt into the wound.

As we travel farther along the continuum of disappointment, we find weightier expectations and more serious risks of hurt and disappointment. Family relationships carry especially high expectations. Children, spouses, siblings, and parents hold the power to hurt us precisely because we inherently trust them to care about us. Close friendships can stimulate and satisfy us, but they can also hurt us deeply when our expectations are shattered. David wrote about being wounded by a trusted friend:

> For it is not an enemy who reproaches me,
> Then I could bear it;
> Nor is it one who hates me who has exalted himself against
> me,
> Then I could hide myself from him.
> But it is you, a man my equal,
> My companion and my familiar friend.
> We who had sweet fellowship together,
> Walked in the house of God in the throng.   **Psalm 55:12-14**

We are not disappointed just by human relationships. We often expect God to provide something we desperately need, but it doesn't happen. We trust him that a child or spouse or friend will change and meet our needs, but the person only moves further away from us. We believe that God will change a part of us that we can't—and won't—talk about, but the dreaded temptation soon seizes us again. The psalmists were not hesitant to express to God their disappointment. David wrote:

> Be gracious to me, O Lord, for I am pining away;
> Heal me, O Lord, for my bones are dismayed.
> And my soul is greatly dismayed;
> But thou, O Lord—how long?
>
> I am weary with my sighing;
> Every night I make my bed swim,
> I dissolve my couch with my tears.
> My eye has wasted away with grief;
> It has become old because of all my adversaries.
>
> Psalm 6:2-3, 6-7

All of us experience pain and disappointment in our interactions with other people as well as in our relationship with God. When another person's choices hurt us, we need to put our rusty conflict resolution skills to work. Most of us try to avoid confrontation at all costs, but an environment is not truly safe if those who live in it can't resolve the inevitable problems. We easily "blow off" the first few unresolved hurts of a young friendship, dating relationship, job, or family. "Oh, just forget it," we say to ourselves. "It's not that big of a deal." "He didn't mean what he said." "She couldn't help it." "You wouldn't believe what he's been through lately."

While these reasonable statements seem to help a little, the wound grows deeper with each passing day. Fresh offenses then compound the initial wound. Now the risk of confronting the real issue seems too threatening, so we continue to repress, excuse, and minimize. We may be able to continue a masquerade of love and peace on the surface, but underneath, our anger at the offender builds and our fear of being hurt continues to grow.

People respond to these wounds in various ways. Some want to withdraw to avoid the risk of hurt. Others feel a strong drive to succeed and please people to prove themselves. Our confidence may wane. Fuzzy perception may lead us to believe we're totally innocent victims or horrible victimizers—or both. In the extreme, our lives can be dominated by feelings of shame, helplessness, hopelessness, and worthlessness.

We all need the courage to say, "I'm sorry. I was wrong." Or, "Can we talk about what just happened between us?" While always uncomfortable for the moment, such words provide a vital ingredient in creating a safe and trustworthy relationship. In that sort of context, people feel protected by a safety net of honest, loving communication.

OUR CRAVING FOR SAFETY

A safe environment provides fertile soil in which to grow self-confidence and, ultimately, emotional and relational health. Generally, the safer we feel, the less our lives will be shaped and dominated by fear and shame.

I recently saw this dynamic played out in the life of my son, Taylor, who is eleven years old. As I pulled into the school parking lot to pick him up after soccer practice one day, I noticed several other parents leaving with their children. I drove up to a group of boys waiting on the sidewalk, expecting to find Taylor. But he wasn't there.

I rolled down the window. "Todd, do you know where Taylor is?"

"No, I haven't seen him since practice."

"Good grief," I grumbled. "Where is he?"

I got out of the car and walked over to another field to see if he had gotten into a pickup game. No Taylor.

I crossed paths with the assistant coach. "Andy, do you know where Taylor is?"

"I haven't seen him since practice ended."

Haven't I heard that before? I was starting to get a bit perturbed, and concerned, too. My pace quickened as I walked to the next field.

About a hundred yards away, I spotted Taylor with several boys who were kicking their soccer balls against the side of the school building. I hollered to him and he started toward me. As Taylor walked closer, I decided not to say anything, yet.

"Hi, Son. How was practice?"

We chatted about soccer and school until we had completed the long trek back to the car. On the way home, I tried to encourage Taylor and still communicate my desire that he be more attentive to little details—like being somewhere in the county when I arrived to pick him up.

"Son, some children would be really afraid to miss their parents when they drove up." I explained how fear of rejection motivates obedience and guarantees compliance in some families. "Some kids are so afraid of being yelled at that they wouldn't think of making their parents wait or look for them. But, Taylor, you don't seem to have that fear."

My son's expression told me that he understood what I was talking about. "You've helped out in that way, Dad. I don't feel afraid because when I mess up, you don't yell at me... much." I was touched and encouraged that Taylor felt safe, and glad that I hadn't jumped all over him at the earliest opportunity.

Three types of trust and mistrust. When we don't feel safe, our ability to trust and our ability to discern who is trustworthy can become distorted to an extreme. We develop all kinds of defense mechanisms to assure our safety. We try to control people's access to us so they can't hurt us. We feel driven to prove our value and win respect. We hide from people so we won't be rejected. We avoid risks so we won't fail. We distort truth by idealizing, minimizing, excusing, and repressing reality. We try to structure virtually every aspect of our lives and every relationship to block pain and gain love and respect. All of these responses flow from our craving for safety.

The yearning for safety becomes so strong in some people that they trust even those who behave in threatening ways. This is *blind trust*. These individuals cannot or will not perceive the reality of harsh, abusive, neglectful, and selfish relationships. They do not have the emotional strength to admit the absence of safety. To win the approval they so desperately want, they try to please others, especially those who hurt them.

Others realize that their environment isn't safe, and then hide emotionally and even physically from those who are abrasive or abusive. People who respond with *passive distrust* have given up on others. Their defense against further hurt is to avoid conflict at all cost, to be quiet and nice at all times, to avoid "rocking the boat."

Still others realize their environment isn't safe, but aggressively move toward people to dominate and control. This is *aggressive distrust*. These individuals use their wit, intelligence, anger, social skills, and double messages to draw people close enough to control them, but keep them far enough away to avoid the risks of intimacy.

These three types of trust and mistrust obviously affect our relationship with God. Those who trust blindly typically expect God to take responsibility for their every need—with little activity on their part. Those who distrust tend to feel distant from God or try to manipulate him to do their will.

These distorted views of the truth can lead us to selectively choose passages of Scripture to bolster our particular perspective. And then we're left wondering why God doesn't do what we expect (or demand!) of him, why he seems silent and aloof when we need him, and why we can work so hard to please him, yet still feel so hurt or driven or angry.

A WAY OUT

"All that stuff sounds great," Rachel told me after several of us talked about these three kinds of trust. "I can see exactly where I've been in my relationships: I was passive with my dominating husband, but I dominate my children and friends. It's all very clear—too clear! You don't understand how ingrained these ways are with me. I don't omit too many people. I don't see how I can change, but I want to. What do I do now?"

I went on to describe a fourth type of trust which produces the proper balance in our relationships. *Perceptive trust* entails the ability to objectively discern the trustworthiness of others and the capacity to take the risk of trusting them. People who have learned to exercise perceptive trust grow in wisdom over time and through many experiences, gradually learning when, how, and whom to trust. But they always remember that only God remains 100 percent trustworthy, as well as totally outside of their control.

As Rachel learned more about trust, she understood more clearly how these patterns had developed. She saw how she passively withdrew from oppressive, strong people to avoid the risk of being hurt, but also how she herself oppressed relatively weaker people. Rachel became increasingly honest about her defenses. And slowly, she learned to take the risk of speaking the truth to stronger people and to value those she had previously dominated.

When I bumped into Rachel at the grocery store one day, she told me about a recent incident with her boss. "I used to cower before him whenever he was angry. After that I'd feel about as much anger toward myself as I did toward him. And today he was in his usual Attila the Hun mood and I didn't hide or back away. I simply spoke the truth to him about the order he asked me to research. I didn't yell. I just told him the facts."

"How did he respond to you?" I asked her.

"At first, he looked a little surprised, but took it just fine. In fact, he didn't explode or anything."

"How did *you* feel about it?"

"It may seem like a little thing to some people, but today was an important day in my life. I was excited as I spoke to him, and I was scared, too! But I feel more alive than I have in years. My fear has kept me immobile and numb, but I'm learning to relate to people very differently than in the past. I don't want to be passive anymore. I want to have *real* relationships—whatever that means!" she laughed.

Rachel was learning to make better choices about who to trust, how to trust, and how trusting perceptively affects her relationships. As you read the rest of this book, I hope you will recognize the patterns of trust in your own life. This understanding can help you learn how to find safety, develop clearer perception, begin to take appropriate risks, and cultivate healthier, stronger relationships. In the chapters ahead we will try to answer the following questions:

- How is trust established in healthy, normal childhood development?

- How do relationships with friends, spouse, employers, and others affect our ability to trust?

- How do stressful relationships erode or shatter our ability to trust?

- How do we develop patterns of blind trust, passive distrust, and/or aggressive distrust to protect ourselves?

- How is every relationship in our lives affected, including our relationship with God?

- How can we rebuild damaged trust?

- How can we develop perceptive trust?

Each chapter concludes with several questions and exercises. I encourage you not to simply "fill in the blanks," but to thoughtfully reflect and consider the principles addressed in that particular chapter. The complex issue of trust undergirds every relationship. As you pursue bonds based on honesty and integrity, whatever time and effort you expend in the study of trust will be rewarded with fresh insights and clearer direction.

❖ ❖ ❖

Take Time to Reflect

1. During what periods of your life did you feel safe and secure?

2. How did feeling safe affect your moods, your willingness to take risks, your self-confidence, and your relationships?

3. What are some results of trusting an untrustworthy person?

4. What are some results of not trusting a trustworthy person?

2

Retracing Your Steps

A FEW MONTHS AGO, I was asked to help resolve a long-standing conflict between two church deacons. When I met with Phil, he detailed all of the errors, shortcomings, weaknesses, and sins of the other man. He discussed Ray's need to control, his rigidity, his inability to communicate, his poor relationships, and his unfaithfulness. I thought he was going to blame his colleague for everything from acne to the national debt!

As Phil finished this rather dismal assessment of Ray's character, I asked him a question. "What was your relationship with your parents like?" The man looked stunned, as if my words came from left field, out of the blue, in Swahili. I could see the mental wheels turning; he was wondering how in the world this question related to our conversation.

Phil then recounted his childhood with a harsh, abusive father and a passive mother. As I continued to probe, a thoroughly painful past came to light. After getting married in 1948, his dad fought in Korea as an infantry sergeant. In the invasion at Inchon, some of his men were captured. The stories of North Korean and Chinese atrocities toward prisoners of war haunted the sergeant. He imagined the horror they might be experiencing. And he felt responsible for their capture.

Deeply affected by the war, Phil's father returned a changed man. He seldom laughed or joked with friends. In fact, he had very few friends. He often exploded into a violent rage with little provocation. Soon everyone learned that it was best to just stay away—which is exactly what Phil did.

This man's wife was devastated by the change in her husband. At first she tried to understand, to comfort, and to help, but his persistent anger finally persuaded her to stop trying. This woman lived in perpetual hopelessness, going through the motions but empty of life and love. Because of her own desperation, she couldn't give her son what he needed.

In this environment, Phil had no one to trust but himself. His dad was tough and mean, his mother emotionally sterile. He had to make it on his own. Some people might crack and become as helpless as his mom. Not Phil. He would prove himself to be tough.

After hearing Phil's story, I asked him, "Do you see any connections between your conflict with Ray and your difficult childhood experiences?"

He thought for a few minutes, then he shook his head, "No, I don't see any at all."

Obviously, both parties were at fault in the conflict. Both deacons had contributed to their unresolved bitterness. Phil, however, failed to see that his angry, controlling, intimidating style led ultimately to more conflict, not resolution. Similar patterns were reflected in his lifestyle: eighty-hour work weeks, shallow relationships, emotional discontent, with a lot of people left in his wake who felt intimidated and discarded.

Phil's propensity toward blaming and controlling, his unwillingness to listen, and his inability to admit his sins and shortcomings could be traced to his family background. He didn't feel safe in that environment because he wasn't safe! His current behaviors and beliefs were, to some degree, a product of the defenses he had acquired early in life to protect himself. He intuitively learned that he could trust only himself. Others, he surmised, either hurt you or find you too weak to care. Driven to prove himself, Phil was unable to see or accept his own weaknesses. They were too threatening to him. But he was quick to see the weaknesses of others, especially people much like his mom and dad.

Ray reminded Phil of his dad. The emotions of his youth surfaced again, with all the repressed hurt and anger subconsciously focused on his fellow deacon. Phil knew better than to lash out in anger, so he subtly criticized Ray both privately and publicly.

Phil reflects many of the characteristics of those who have never learned to trust and who try to cope by aggressively dominating others: rigid self-reliance, intimidation, lack of self-perception, constant criticism of others, and suspicion of others' motives. How can we find the root of such destructive patterns in our own lives?

LOOKING BACK

The genesis of our ability or inability to trust occurs very early in our lives. In fact, we learn about trust from birth by receiving verbal and nonverbal messages from those who take care of us. As we go through the formative years of childhood, our relationships with adults continue to affect our perceptions and trust behaviors.

At any point in life, sudden and dramatic life changes—as painful as the death of a sibling or as wonderful as marrying a loving, mature person—can profoundly influence our trust quotient. In fact, these later experiences usually bring to the surface the perceptions and behaviors we developed early in life.

Many authorities recognize identifiable stages of intellectual, emotional, relational, and physical development. One of the most widely noted paradigms is the eight stages of ego development proposed by Erik Erikson. For our purposes, we will focus on the first two of Erikson's developmental stages: trust versus mistrust, and autonomy versus shame and doubt. By synthesizing the implications of these first two, we will distill the other six into one single stage: identity. In these three stages, we can examine the establishment of trust in others, trust in self, and the results of validated trust.

1. *Trust versus mistrust* (birth to one year): establishing trust in others versus suspicion and wariness.
2. *Autonomy versus shame and doubt* (about one to three years): establishing trust in self versus insecurity and lack of confidence.
3. *Identity* (childhood, adolescence, and early adulthood): implications of trusting or not trusting (the establishment of roles, sexual identity, intimacy, communication skills, and purpose).

Whenever individuals are encouraged to look back to their childhood experience to help them understand their present adult behaviors, some people wonder, "Why look back? My childhood is ancient history. It's over. I want to understand how to cope with my boss (or spouse or child or friend or whoever) *today!*"

Good question. We don't look back just to complete some abstract, academic, psychological exercise. We don't do it in order to find someone to blame for our present difficulties. A healthy, objective analysis of our past helps us to see patterns in our behavior which have been shaped by important relationships and events. You may realize that your current responses are the product of many, seemingly insignificant, events which slowly come together like a one-thousand-piece jigsaw puzzle. Or you may learn that your personal puzzle contains a few large pieces representing traumas or blessings: perhaps a sister's drowning accident, a delightful relationship with a loving grandparent, or a long repressed incident of sexual molestation.

We often find our adult behaviors confusing. "Why in the world do I always treat her that way?" "I hate it when I wilt and give in! Why do I do that?" we ask in disgust. We need insight. We need wisdom. We need to resolve those baffling difficulties that keep us hung up and prevent us from enjoying honest, loving relationships and meaningful work.

Scripture encourages us to "consider our ways" so that we can learn and grow. The patterns of trusting blindly or being passive or aggressive when we don't trust at all are usually deeply ingrained. Surface solutions seldom work. Looking back will help us deal with the present much more effectively.

Let's take a look, then, at our initial stages of development.

NAKED AND HELPLESS

The first stage of development is almost entirely instinctive and intuitive. The totally dependent infant responds like a veritable sponge, soaking up the unintelligible words, tone of voice, facial expression, physical closeness, general sense of safety, and the provision of basic needs. By singing, talking, kissing, smiling at each new movement, cuddling, and providing food and protection, the parent communicates to the child, "You are safe here. You can trust me."

In this pre-verbal stage, babies learn to trust when someone provides the basic needs of food, warmth, safety, and nurture. Proper development requires not only physical provision but emotional bonding as well. If caregivers fail to meet these basic needs, children learn that others aren't safe and can't be trusted. Abuse, neglect, and perfunctory treatment create an intuitive lack of trust in the child.

Extended families of the past typically provided a very safe environment, with more intensive nurturing for infants. Today's mobile, two-income, fast-paced society renders many grandparents, aunts, and uncles unavailable to help care for children. Parents increasingly turn to unrelated "mother substitutes," often a necessity for single mothers who must earn a living for themselves and their children. Many professionals, however, point out that these substitutes are not nearly as effective in creating a sense of safety and trust.

While parents need to spend enough time with children, the *quality* of their care also proves to be a significant determinant.

For example, studies have linked unconditional acceptance by the mother to emotional, social, and intellectual growth, while conditionally-loved children often exhibit inordinate guilt, hostility, and anxiety with intrapersonal and interpersonal consequences.[1]

The extremes of neglect or smothering can produce either defiant self-reliance and isolation without the skills necessary for meaningful attachments, or else extreme dependence, indecision, and passivity. Although quite different outwardly, both sets of behavior are based in mistrust and insecurity.

The good news is parenting need not be perfect to produce a trust-building environment, but just "good enough," as Judith Viorst explains in *Necessary Losses*. "Good enough" parenting is balanced and consistent. Children are usually able to assimilate good enough affirmation, provision, protection, time, and care.

Children receive a crucial message through consistent nurturing: "You don't have to be afraid. You don't have to fend for yourself. You can trust us to be strong and kind." This message continues to have a strong impact on relationships with authority figures throughout a person's life. Ultimately, of course, this initial perception also influences a person's view of God.

In our earliest years, we instinctively determine that those over us are either for us, against us, or maybe just don't care. We transfer those conclusions to other authorities. If our trust was validated early in life, we may become comfortable in relating to authority with honest communication. If not, we may become suspicious of authority, rebel in defiance, give up in apathy, go on a crusade to change it, or withdraw from it in fear.

To put it simply, if children feel safe, they will learn to trust. If they feel consistently threatened, they will begin to develop defensive measures to protect themselves from further hurt.

I need only to look out the window at my home to see examples of this principle. One ten-year-old girl comes from a home with loving, attentive parents. She relates easily to everybody, including adults. When I talk to her, she looks me in the eye and communicates freely with me. She obviously feels secure. Her trust level is high.

Another neighborhood story isn't so pleasant. A nine-year-old boy's parents are aloof, cold, and detached. He's left alone most of the time. He uses foul language openly. He picks on even the smallest children and relentlessly seeks revenge for the slightest perceived offense. He rarely laughs, except when someone else is hurt. I've tried to talk to this boy, to get to know him and befriend him, but he looks down, gives short answers, and seems uncomfortable. This nine-year-old has already developed a tough, dominating, intimidating defense to control other people, but under that steel-plated exterior is a scared little boy.

This initial stage of trust development, then, provides a crucial phase in our emotional, relational, and spiritual lives. It is the foundation which determines many issues:

- How we interpret people and events (as threats or challenges).

- How we relate to others (desperately needing them to fill the hole in our lives, avoiding them out of fear, or giving and receiving with honesty, love, and wisdom).

- Our primary purpose in life (to prove ourselves, to avoid pain, or to love and serve thankfully).[2]

Many experts believe that this phase of development is the most important, as it is the first. Each stage of development must be successfully completed before going on to the next. If this first stepping stone of development is missed, we will miss the rest as well.

LEARNING TO TRUST YOURSELF

The second developmental stage, autonomy, focuses on self-confidence. Some Christians think of self-confidence as wrong and sinful. In the extreme, it is. But appropriate self-confidence plays a vital role throughout our lives. Being confident in ourselves means placing a proper valuation on our abilities and our skill in using them. The extremes of cockiness on one end of the spectrum and fearful indecision on the other are both destructive to ourselves and to meaningful relationships.

Self-confidence is a synonym for self-control. If all goes well, children develop a sense of self-control (the ability to make their own decisions within limits) without self-contempt (the sense of shame and doubt in their abilities). As children assert their independence and parents work to set limits, this second developmental stage tends to be full of experimentation and trial and error.

A toddler's quest for autonomy often tests the limits of a parent's patience, but it also provides some humorous incidents. My wife, Joyce, recently found an old cassette tape we made when Catherine and Taylor were little. One side was taped on Christmas morning when Catherine was about two and a half. We had bought the children a toy that could be assembled only by three NASA scientists.

The tape had captured my primeval guttural noises as I tried to make sense of the several billion pieces and twelve-pound instruction manual. Over the sounds of my grumbling, the tape also picked up Catherine's voice as she looked over the mess: "Move, Daddy. I do it. Move, Daddy. I do it." (To tell you the truth, she probably could have done as well as I did!) Toddlers forcefully assert their autonomy and self-confidence. They know they're right!

The other side of the tape was recorded about eight or nine months later. Taylor was two and we were singing into the tape player for posterity's sake. As we began a song, Taylor stopped us. "It's... it's... it's not on."

Joyce gently showed him, "See, Taylor, the red light is on. That means the machine is working. Come on now, let's sing a song!"

"But, but, but it's not on, Mommy," he insisted.

"Yes, it is. Look, Son, look at the light. That means it's recording us right now."

"No. No, it's not on. I turn it on."

Joyce figured out a solution. She turned it off and then let Taylor turn it back on.

"Now, you see. It's on now. Let's sing."

To Taylor, the tape recorder wasn't on until *he* turned it on.

In the autonomy-building stage, children need balance from their parents and other caregivers. They need sufficient encouragement, discipline, affection, and limits on their freedom. Their insistence on making their own decisions needs to be affirmed and praised when they succeed. When they fail or when they insist on doing it their way for the seven hundredth time in one hour, the parent's reaction needs to be calm, consistent, and firm.

When caregivers fail to provide this balance, children internalize the neglect, smothering attention, or anger. They assume, "There's something wrong with me. I'm a bad person." Instead of self-confidence, children experience self-doubt, feelings of inadequacy, and repressed development of learning skills. They develop self-contempt rather than self-control.

As in the first stage of learning trust, the extremes of neglect and smothering on the part of caregivers produce extremes in a child's self-perception and behavior. Those who are smothered with attention and not given the freedom to decide and fail on their own may learn to see themselves as only an extension of others—without a sense of separateness. As a consequence, these individuals don't see themselves as capable and adequate. They believe others have to make decisions for them.

On the other hand, children who are neglected or abused may see themselves as autonomous and isolated, without substantial emotional connections to others. They too internalize the stress around them and feel self-contempt.

If our parents neglected or smothered us, we may treat our children the same way, or we may do the opposite. One woman had been verbally and physically abused by her father. She determined not to do that to her own children, but she didn't know how to treat them with love and respect. She ended up withdrawing from them. She was abused by her dad; in turn, she avoided her own children.

The process of trial and error which characterizes this stage of life creates a strong need for reassurance. Children take significant risks to be separate, to make their own choices. Such behavior often threatens insecure parents. They don't understand the dynamics of the child's anger and feel the need to condemn and control. As parents, some of us need to be more attentive and give more guidance and feedback. Others need to "chill out" and let children have room to grow and try new things without constant instruction and condemnation.

In this stage, children need a lot of affirmation just for trying, whether or not they succeed. Our reassurance gives them confidence to try again, to develop a sense of healthy independence, to strengthen their abilities. Parenting is an art. It requires patience and skill to give children enough attention to impart reassurance but not so much that they become dependent and indecisive, robbed of the adventure of being competent adults.

You may see yourself as similar to one of the children in the examples above, or perhaps to one of the parents. Remember that our goal is to understand, not to condemn, to gain wisdom so we can make better choices. In later chapters, we will consider the specific choices and changes we can make, but first let's try to understand how we build on this foundation of trust and autonomy to form our identity.

BUILT ON SOLID ROCK OR SHIFTING SAND

If they have been soundly constructed, the two building blocks of trust and autonomy form a stable foundation for the rest of our development. Trust in others and appropriate self-confidence motivate and shape the direction of our growth. The remaining childhood years encompass the formation of roles, sexual identity, and personal strengths. Adulthood holds the possibility of true intimacy if two people with established, secure identities commit themselves to one another in marriage. Productivity along with a sense of posterity and eternity are the final hallmarks of the developmental process.

Adolescence is a pivotal period in the development of trust. Tremendous pressures mark these years: physiological growth, hormonal changes, social inclusion or ostracism, and experimentation in virtually every aspect of life. At this stage, identity is formed. The risks are high, with the rewards or punishments often experienced daily and intensely.

The teen years are difficult even for the most stable and secure person. Many adolescents, however, lack the wisdom and maturity to process this stress. Previous family instability or current crises may have eroded their confidence. They often feel hurt, angry, and threatened, but typically internalize these difficulties rather than resolve them.

In his book, *Helping the Struggling Adolescent,* Les Parrot, a professor at Seattle Pacific University, describes potentially passive responses: "Adolescents with low self-esteem may be distractible, shy, withdrawn, inhibited, or anxious. They are more likely to daydream and want to be in situations with minimal competition. They have few, if any, expectations of success. They often lack a sense of belongingness and fear new experiences."

Dr. Parrot then describes the opposite response adolescents may have toward the same feelings of inferiority: "To protect themselves from further pain they erect barriers. They may exhibit a disproportionate amount of hostility, criticism, bragging, suspiciousness, or denial. It is too risky for these struggling adolescents to be exposed to additional hurt, so they wear psychic armor."[3]

All of us possess some sense of identity, but sadly, many of us cling tightly to a stunted, distorted sense of personhood. To the extent that our trust in others has been invalidated so that we lack self-confidence and perception, our identity is based on what others think of us. Those of us who blindly trust become an extension of others with whom we are enmeshed. Their identities (thoughts, feelings, behaviors) become our own. Those of us who don't trust become isolated, without the emotional connections and confidence necessary to establish and develop a healthy self-concept.

Identity development, however, is predicated upon our sense of security and the implications of our ability to trust others and ourselves. Many of us have developed elaborate, concrete defenses to protect ourselves precisely because we haven't felt safe and we haven't learned to trust. We typically solve life's problems by making our defenses stronger than ever to avoid being hurt again.

Instead, we need to look at the reasons *why* we defend ourselves so vigorously and *why* we feel so vulnerable. Only then can we develop practical strategies for dealing with the real problems instead of wasting so much energy reorganizing and refortifying our surface defenses.

We have examined the ways in which our early life experiences and growing up years affect our ability to trust others and to form meaningful relationships. These experiences encourage or hinder our capacity to trust wisely. More specifically, they help to form our competence, our relationships, our ability to resolve problems, our capacity to be honest, to love, to grieve, and to laugh.

How solid is our trust foundation? How many wounds have never been resolved? How do we deal with traumatic events in our lives? Trust can be shattered by something that hits like a huge tidal wave, leaving shock and devastation. Or it may be slowly eroded by consistent criticism, neglect, smothering, or double messages—like a sluggish river inexorably altering the landscape, moving silt, and changing course.

❖ ❖ ❖

Take Time to Reflect

1. Write a "trust history" about your father. Who were the trustworthy people in his life? How did they affect him? How old was he when he was around them? Who were the untrustworthy people in his life?

2. Write a "trust history" about your mother. Who were the trustworthy people in her life? How did they affect her? How old was she when she was around them? Who were the untrustworthy people in her life?

3. Write your own "trust history." Who were the trustworthy people in your life? How did they affect you? How old were you when you were around them? Who were the untrustworthy people in your life?

4. Who are the people in your life now who are generally trustworthy? How do they affect you?

5. Who are the people in your life now who are generally untrustworthy? How do they affect you?

3

The Shattering of Trust

AFTER A HAPPY AND STABLE CHILDHOOD, Jill fell in love with the man of her dreams. Harold had been a football star in high school and was now a successful businessman. He was handsome, witty, and charming. Everyone in town thought they were the ideal couple. Jill told me the tragic truth: "The day after we married, Harold changed—and I don't mean 'a little.' All the charm and affection he showed me when we were engaged vanished. I never saw it coming."

Jill's memories of those days brought back the shock and horror. Her eyes glazed a bit, but she continued. "When my husband hit me that day, I thought, *He's just having a really bad day!* I couldn't believe what was happening. Well, maybe I *wouldn't* believe it. For over a year, Harold cursed me, hit me—but never in places anybody could see, or at least I could cover it up with long sleeves. I didn't tell anybody. Nobody would believe me, or at least that's what I thought.

"For a year, I lived in this silent nightmare. I told everybody how wonderful my husband was. When my closest friends could tell something was wrong, I told them it was my hormones. After a while, they didn't believe me, so I avoided them. In that year, the happiness and joy of my life died. A close friend finally dragged the truth out of me. Harold became absolutely furious when he found out I had told someone. I left that day."

We continued to talk. "I'm not sure I can ever trust anybody ever again—especially a man. I'm suspicious of everything they say and do. Maybe I shouldn't be, but I'm never going to go through that again. Staying away is the best way to keep from being hurt again."

Our continued progress in building on the foundation established early in life can be brought to a screeching halt by a traumatic event. A couple may learn they can't have children. A single mother may lose her job without warning. A best friend may move across the country. An employee of thirty-five years may learn the refinery is closing just a couple of years before his retirement. A competent executive may be bypassed for a promotion in favor of a young hot shot. Some trust-jolting tragedies occur only once in our lives: a father's death in a hunting accident, a sister's paralysis from a car wreck, a parent moving across the country after a divorce, or a home being razed by fire. Childhood traumas, however, more often entail repeated offenses in which the personal devastation deepens, leaving a gaping wound that continues to fester.

In our adults lives, traumatic events may be singular incidents or they may form part of a consistent pattern. Some of us continue to put ourselves into dangerous situations and relationships where our trust is violated.

Traumas scream, "Danger! You're not safe!" We feel violated, insecure, confused. Our trust in others is shattered. With enough nurturing and support, the wounds can be faced and grieved. Trust can be rebuilt. Sadly, few of us feel safe enough to expose our wounds so that we can feel, grieve, and grow. Instead, we search for safety in any way we can, typically by manipulation, denial, secrecy, or control.

When a shocking experience jolts someone without the stability and strength of affirming relationships, that person can be left feeling like Humpty Dumpty at the bottom of the wall. Let's consider some of the ways in which we might be suddenly knocked off balance.

WHEN TRUST IS BETRAYED

Any time we trust someone to meet a need, we run the risk of disappointment. Betrayal comes in all sizes and shapes, but it always hurts and it always threatens our capacity to trust the next time.

Bill became engrossed in the success of his new business venture. Every minute and every dime were focused on making money. His wife accepted the fact that new companies require extra effort, but after a while Debbie began to wonder. "Can't you take more time with the children now that you're doing so well?" she asked her husband.

"You just don't understand business," Bill muttered as he left for work to pour over some projected sales figures—at ten o'clock at night.

A few months later, Bill calmly told his wife—with the cool detachment of an accountant going over the latest figures, "You and the kids are costing me too much money. I'm going to leave you so you won't drag me down anymore."

Debbie was crushed. She had seen all the signs, but had blindly hoped her husband would change. Instead, Bill had accelerated his drive to get what he wanted. Their marriage ended with a final twist of the knife: he had put the house in his name alone.

Individuals aren't the only source of betrayal. People often feel betrayed by organizations. Al served his company loyally and ably for many years. Then, three years ago, it was sold in a leveraged buy-out. The new owners needed to cut expenses and conducted meetings in secret. Rumors flew. According to a revamped organizational chart, one third of the middle managers lost their jobs. The company didn't use the word "fired," of course. "Early retirement" was suggested for some, while others were referred to a firm which provided outplacement services.

Al was too young to retire, but too old to start over again. In only a few weeks, he had gone from a stable, secure position as a competent and loyal employee to being unceremoniously dumped. His shock was mixed with anger. "They told me I could retire here. They told me I was one of their most valued employees. Then the buy-out. And now this." His eyes grew fierce, "I'll tell you one thing. I'll never believe what some company tells me again! I'll make sure people treat me right from now on!"

Should this man have trusted in a profit-motivated organization to meet his needs? Perhaps not, but the company management had bolstered his expectations by promising to provide for him. When these hopes were dashed, Al felt betrayed.

A third source of betrayal is gossip. Gossip is such a common occurrence that we may not identify it as betrayal. But when someone uses confidential information about us or from us to ingratiate themselves to others, he or she betrays our trust.

Suzanne told me, "Jane has been a good friend of mine for years. We've talked and laughed about a lot of things over the years. A few weeks ago I was discouraged. She asked me what was wrong. I'm usually very private about my family, but I thought it would be good to talk about my problem. I told Jane about my daughter's relationship with a long-haired boy in her class in high school. I was worried sick about her. He played in a rock band, and you know all those stories about drugs and sex. I tried not to imagine what they were doing."

As Suzanne talked about her daughter, the anguish in her face turned to anger. "A few days later, another woman in our church asked me how my daughter's relationship with the 'rock star' was going. 'Fine,' I said quickly. How did she know? I guessed she had seen them together somewhere.

"After a couple of other people asked me about them, I asked, 'Did you see them together?'

"'No,' was the reply. 'Jane asked us to pray for them.'

"'Pray for them!?' I didn't want anybody to know about them or if they found out, I sure didn't want them to know how worried I was. I'll never tell Jane anything else about me, my family, or anything important!"

A betrayal of confidence boils down to a breach of trust, one which isn't easily resolved and often affects other relationships as well. We begin to feel suspicious of those who may actually be trustworthy, and hesitate to entrust ourselves to them until they prove themselves.

LOSS BY DIVORCE, DESERTION, OR DEATH

"I was seven when Mom and Dad divorced," Bonnie told me. "They had been angry at each other before. My brother and sister and I knew there were some problems, but we had no idea they might split up. Mom was devastated and disoriented. After a month or so, we moved to live with my grandparents, but Mom just got worse there. She cried a lot. She couldn't stand for us to even mention Dad. We didn't hear from him for years.

"When I was thirteen, I was interested in a guy. I told my mom that he had asked me out, and she exploded! She told me, 'OK, go ahead! You'll see! Men are all alike—they can't be trusted!' Since the divorce, Mom hasn't trusted men. I guess she's afraid of getting hurt again. The problem is," Bonnie continued, "she didn't have to tell me that. I didn't trust men either, and I still have problems trusting them. I feel confused. I want a relationship so badly, but I always push men away after they show any interest in me."

Bonnie's traumatic experience of her parents' divorce and her father's desertion received regular booster shots from the ways her mother continued to model her own paranoia. Distrust of men became Bonnie's legacy and lifestyle.

Death. Studies suggest that two of the most destructive events we can experience are the death of a spouse and the death of a child.[1] These stresses severely challenge our coping skills and our ability to trust. Julie, a tired, suburban mother of three, sat down for a short break. She had been shopping; she had played with the children; she had paid the bills. Now, she wanted a few minutes of quiet on a hot summer afternoon.

"Watch after your sisters, Robbie," she called to her fifteen-year-old son. "Don't let them get near the pool while I'm inside the house."

While his mom took a nap, Robbie dutifully played with the girls. Then the phone rang. A buddy had gone to a giant water slide with several friends the day before, and now he had the latest scoop about who was dating whom, who broke up with whom, and other juicy tidbits. Robbie quickly became absorbed in every detail. Suddenly, Jill ran in, "Margie's in the pool! She's not swimming! Come quick!"

Robbie ran to the pool and jumped in to grab his sister. With fear filling his eyes, the teenage boy quickly handed her limp form to his mother, who had been awakened by Jill's cry for help. Three-year-old Margie was already blue and lifeless. Emergency personnel quickly answered Julie's phone call. They hoped and prayed for what they had seen on the weekly television program, *Rescue 911:* child near death, professional care, life restored, smiling family.

Not this time: Margie died.

Long after the initial shock wore off, the pain felt almost unbearable. Julie wondered bitterly, *How could God do this to me? It's not fair. It's not right.* The trauma had also shattered trust relationships within the family. Julie tried very hard not to blame Robbie for his lapse of responsibility, but he knew. He knew his mother blamed him and, possibly, would never trust him again. He couldn't trust himself either. He seethed with self-hatred. Five-year-old Jill was a victim of shattered trust, too. She knew her brother had been wrong in not paying attention to them, and the tension and anger in the air seemed almost tangible to her. Somebody could have, should have, prevented her sister's death.

A backyard pool. A few minutes on the phone. A child's attraction to water. A tragedy. A shattered family that refuses to heal and trust again.

SEXUAL AND PHYSICAL ABUSE

"I was six years old when we went to a family reunion," Nancy told me. "We were having a terrific time. Everybody seemed so happy and friendly. Then on the second night during dinner, my uncle started paying a lot of attention to me. I liked it! It felt good. Later that night, I went to bed while the adults danced. My uncle came into my room and lay down on my bed. We talked a long time. I was tired, but I liked the attention. After a while, he said he'd like to rub my back to help me relax so I could sleep better. I liked it. Then he started rubbing my rear. That seemed strange to me. I didn't think it was right, but I liked my uncle.

"When he put his hand in my panties, I felt tremendously confused. *This couldn't be right!* I told myself, but it felt good, too. My uncle kept telling me over and over again in the darkness, 'I'm doing this because I love you. I'm doing this because I love you.' I felt guilty... and happy; dirty... but wanted.

"The next day my uncle hardly looked at me. I felt so hurt and confused. When I went over to him, he grabbed me by the arm and we walked a few feet away from everybody. 'Remember, that's our little secret. Don't tell anybody about it or you'll be sorry.'

"My uncle made it a point to come visit us several times in the next few years. Then he just sort of vanished, moved across the country I guess."

I asked, "Did you ever tell your parents what your uncle did to you?"

"No,... well, one time I tried to bring it up. I asked my mom, 'What if something like that happened to me?' She said she couldn't imagine her own brother doing anything so horrible. She got mad that I even mentioned it, so I never brought it up again."

"Nancy, how did all this affect your ability to trust others?" I questioned her.

"It really confused me. I didn't feel safe telling my parents or anyone else the truth, so I kept it to myself. I felt desired by my uncle, but I felt dirty and ashamed when I was with him, too. Somehow I felt really alive when I was with him but dead after he left. I felt increasingly isolated from my parents because I couldn't tell them what was going on. I felt so many intense and conflicting emotions about my uncle and about myself. Over time, I learned to trust only people who used me. That's all I felt good for. And I would do anything to feel accepted by them."

Physical abuse. Ted told me his sad story of physical abuse. "My dad would come home late every Friday night. Friday was payday. After he'd gotten paid, he would go out drinking with his buddies. I guess he was what they call a 'mean drunk' because he would come home cussing and throwing things.

"I always hid in my room while my older brother and mother tried to calm him down. They would yell and scream at each other. It only happened a couple of times, but sometimes I heard him ask where I was. Pretty soon I'd hear him coming down the hall. He'd barge into my room and ask me something like, 'Why didn't you come out to speak to me when I got home? You don't appreciate your old man, do you?' Then he'd hit me or slap me a few times. When he left, I cried for hours, not so much because my head hurt, but because my own dad hated me!

"My older brothers had been hit by my dad plenty of times. They refused to hide from him when he came home. They'd yell and cuss just as loud as he did. I guess they stored up their anger and needed somebody to take it out on, so they'd take it out on me. At first they 'frogged' me on the arms so nobody could see any bruises. It was a game to them. They'd laugh when I tried to get away; they'd laugh when I finally got away. Sometimes, though, when we were older, they really beat me up badly. I got out of there as fast as I could when I turned sixteen."

I asked Ted, "Where was your mother when all this was going on? Did you tell her? Was she supportive?"

He looked disgusted at my question, "Mom? Supportive? No chance! She had all she could handle with my dad. She didn't want to hear about my brothers being mean to me."

"Ted," I asked him, "you told me you had problems with your employer, and you told me this kind of problem has happened before. Do you see any connection between your home life and your relationship problems at work?"

Looking puzzled, Ted thought for a moment. "What do you mean?"

"Sometimes we generalize," I explained. "We associate certain events in our lives with anyone who reminds us of the people in those events. Many people associate their perspective of their parents with anybody in authority over them—such as employers. If they're afraid of their parents, they might also fear how a boss would treat them, and they might react defensively or quit or expect to be treated unfairly. Do you understand what I'm trying to say?"

"Yeah, I think so. So you're saying the problems I'm having with my unfair boss are like the problems I had with my parents." After a pause, he asked angrily, "Do you think I'm making up this stuff with my boss?"

"No, not at all. I'm just trying to point out that there may be some connection in your perception of authority and your response to your boss."

Suddenly another perceived, unfair authority figure had posed a threat in Ted's life: me! After more discussion, he began to understand the connection. He recalled past reactions to teachers, coaches, and other work supervisors. "I guess I've always thought those people were using me to get whatever they wanted from me. I guess I've always been suspicious of authority."

We all need to be cautious and observant before we entrust ourselves, our time, and our abilities to people or organizations. On the other hand, we need to avoid making the blanket assumption that everyone has a vendetta against us. Our defensiveness will only hinder the possible development of a trust relationship.

MULTIPLE WOUNDS

As members of a fallen race, all of us experience various disappointments and hurts throughout life, but some of us suffer the blows of multiple traumas. Each singly would not crush us, but taken together, they can leave us oppressed and devastated.

A friend of mine grew up in an especially harsh and critical environment. "My sister could do no wrong," Patti explained, "and I could do nothing right. Everything I said and did was criticized. If I set the table, the fork wasn't quite right. When I played in the yard and left a toy, I got yelled at. When I started dating, my boyfriends weren't good enough. You name it, it was wrong."

My friend married a man much like her dad. Nothing Patti did was good enough: her cooking, her cleaning, the way she handled the children, the television shows she watched, her hairstyle, her clothes... anything.

This victim role was perpetuated at work. Even though Patti is quite skilled, she somehow seemed to get on the bad side of her employers. She moved from job to job. "I'm doing all I can," she bemoaned. "What's wrong with them?"

Meanwhile, Patti's children have internalized the tension, attacks, and reactions. They can't explain the chronic shortage of money, work struggles, in-law problems, and all the rest, but they sense it and feel it. Her children acted out their fear and anger in defiance and disobedience, obstacles which further eroded Patti's self-confidence.

No matter how incredible this self-destructive pattern sounds, many of the walking wounded repeat it over and over again. Some of us actually perpetuate the series of traumas which hurt us so deeply. The only role we understand, the only choices we know to make, the only perspective we have of ourselves, is that of a victim. We subconsciously look for others to control us, and we endure harsh treatment in exchange for the relative comfort of letting someone control how we think, feel, and act. It's what we've always known so it feels comfortable, more comfortable than change, growth, and health.

Of course, some people experience multiple traumas through no fault of their own. One man experienced the death of a child, followed a year later by his parents' death in a car wreck, and the loss of his job a month later. On top of all that, he found out that his wife had cancer only a year and a half after that.

Individual events threaten our ability to trust. Multiple wounds bludgeon it. People who experience such devastation often draw negative conclusions about the trustworthiness of people and God. The empirical evidence seems to support their grim conclusion.

INDIRECT WOUNDS

Some people feel traumatized when they witness verbal or physical abuse inflicted on a family member or someone else close to them. Jennifer's parents seldom yelled at her, but they frequently screamed at each other and her brother. "You're my little angel," her mother would reassure her. "I don't know why your father and your brother are such jerks, but you always understand me."

Even though these verbal attacks were never directed at her, the intense environment of stress and hatred caused Jennifer to feel unsafe. She unconsciously developed the defense mechanism of trusting untrustworthy people anyway. If she *believed* them to be safe, perhaps they would actually *be* safe. The young girl also coped through denial, never talking about the turmoil in the family. "Oh, that's just the way they are," Jennifer laughed to a friend who asked about her belligerent parents. "They don't really mean anything by it. A lot of families argue a lot more than ours. Our family is pretty normal."

Another type of indirect wound occurs when another family member experiences a major trauma. One man I know had a brother who was diagnosed with multiple sclerosis. His parents focused their attention and energy almost entirely on the afflicted sibling. The shock of his brother's illness and the pain of his parents' neglect took their toll.

Joan's father suffered a serious stroke when she was in high school, which meant that her mother had to go to work to support the family. When Mom was at home, her attention was focused on her husband's needs. Throughout her formative and volatile high school years, Joan was effectively parentless due to sudden trauma.

In both these cases, the individual who didn't need as much help was neglected. The message they heard was, "Either help or get out of the way. You and your needs aren't important!" The deep feelings of hurt and anger were then coupled with a sense of shame.

Traumas come in all degrees. Even seemingly minor ones can devastate a person who has little emotional strength and stability. Beth explained an event which occurred when she was eleven. "I loved my dog so much. Shelly was kind of a mutt, but I didn't care. My family had moved so many times that Shelly was my only real friend. I was afraid to make new friends each place we went because I didn't want to get hurt when we left.

"One day Shelly was across the street. I called her to come to me. She looked up and started running to me. She never saw the car that hit her. When Mom saw that Shelly was dead, she just said, 'That dog was a mutt anyway. We'll get you another one.'

"That day I decided not to get attached to anything or anybody the rest of my life. It hurt too much. I became just like my mother. That was the way Mom handled everybody's pain, including her own! 'Get over it. Be tough.' Mom couldn't get close to people. I guess all the moves made my mother think that relationships weren't worth it. The break-offs hurt too much, so she hardened herself. Relationships and possessions were expendable. Mom said, 'We'll get you another dog,' like it was a broken dish that could be replaced in a few minutes. I didn't want another dog. I wanted Shelly!"

I asked Beth, "How do you think your home environment, the moving, and your dog's death have affected your trust in God?"

After a few moments of reflection, Beth answered, "I know God loves me. Jesus wouldn't have died for me if he didn't love me a lot, but I guess I've always had a kind of arm's-length relationship with God. I try to do the things he wants me to... but I don't feel close to him very often at all." She paused. "I guess I'm afraid that if I get close, I'll get hurt again."

TRUST CAN BE SHATTERED AT ANY AGE

One of my friends has been battling depression for several years. Jeb's pastor, who is experienced in counseling, has tried to help this man uncover some of the causes of his deep sense of loss. When asked about his childhood, Jeb said, "My folks are great. They can't be more supportive and I really enjoy being with them."

The pastor probed a little deeper. "What about when you were little? Tell me about your family then."

"Oh, when I was really young, my father was a very angry man. I don't remember much, but I do remember being very afraid of him. But that all changed when I was about six. That's when Dad became a Christian, and he's been great since then!"

Who knows whether or not my friend's father really changed so dramatically. Jeb is unwilling to talk about his dad's impact on his life except in glowing terms. Perhaps Jeb's depression stems from some other source which still remains buried, but a father's tantrums create fear in a young boy's heart. Perhaps the damage had never been repaired.

We can be wounded later in life as well. Those of us who trust blindly hang on to the hope that parent, friend, spouse, or boss will somehow come through and meet our needs—even when these people have proven over and over again to be untrustworthy. In clinging to this "hopeless hope," we continually overlook blatant injustices, gross misbehavior, and loud signals that our trust is unfounded and unwise. A day of reckoning usually arrives, however, when the unpalatable truth overwhelms our denial. When blind trust is shattered, we drift—or are catapulted—to the other end of the spectrum toward suspicion and distrust.

Bob would never forget the point of reckoning in his own life. "I grew up in an alcoholic family, but I thought all the hurt and anger, all the self-pity and rescuing, were normal because I'd never seen anything else. After I graduated from college, I got a good job. I was sailing along, but a couple of years later my life came apart. My girlfriend dumped me. My alcoholic mother told people that her drinking was all my fault. And I got a new boss who was a tyrant. Nothing I did was good enough for him. All this at one time blew my world apart!

"I had always expected God to protect me from problems too big for me. I trusted him. I believed him. But he let me down. That was the biggest shock to me: that God wouldn't come through when I needed him. I used to trust everybody. Now I trust nobody—especially God."

Our trust in people and in God can be shattered in a flash, in an instant of trauma. Many of us, however, experience these deeper wounds in the midst of a threatening or unsupportive environment. Rather than being shattered, our sense of trust, autonomy, and identity has been slowly eroding over many years.

We may have felt devalued or forced to continually meet

others' needs while our own needs were neglected. We may have had to play some role to block pain and win approval. Perhaps others always made our choices for us. To some degree, the level and quality of nurturing we received just wasn't enough.

Whatever the source of pain, our trust can slowly erode over a confusing and painful period of weeks, months, and years. We vaguely sense our own foundation being washed out from under us, but still precariously maintain our balance. We keep hoping the bad dream will end, and then wake up to the awful realization that the situation is even worse than we feared. Let's go on to consider how this erosion of trust can happen.

❖ ❖ ❖

Take Time to Reflect

1. If you have experienced traumatic events, how did you respond (feel, think, act) immediately afterward?

2. How did you respond a month later?

3. How did you respond a year later?

4. Do you see any pattern or progression in your responses? If so, how would you describe it?

4

The Erosion of Trust

MANY OF US never experience the severity of trauma commonly recounted on *Oprah* or *Donahue*. We feel empty, hurt, and angry, but we can't point to any specific catastrophic events in our lives which would validate and justify our pain. And so we heap shame on top of everything else. Shouldn't we be happier? Shouldn't we be able to form closer friendships? We constantly compare ourselves to others and come up short, so we either try harder or else give up in despair.

Some of us have experienced both the tidal wave and the river, the shattering and the erosion of trust. We continue to feel both shock and confusion, both hurt and shame.

"My husband and I had a very healthy, happy, and normal physical relationship, I guess," Mary related. "He's an executive, and he's done very well in the company with promotions, bonuses, and all that. By the time we were in our mid-forties, he had become a vice president. He was getting all kinds of awards. I guess he was feeling pretty good about himself."

Mary's eyes dropped. She looked sad. "I guess with all the new people fawning over him, some of the women caught his eye. And he caught theirs. All the money and promotions and awards were exciting. Our whole family was proud of him. But one day I realized that we hadn't had sex in a week, then two weeks, then a month. And he seemed too busy to hug me. And he didn't kiss me—oh, maybe a peck, but not the real thing.

"I felt hurt, but I realized I may not be as attractive as I used to be, so I got some new clothes. I fixed my hair. I really tried to look nice for him. But nothing changed. Maybe, I thought, I'd better initiate a sexual advance toward him before we lose touch with each other completely. He didn't respond. I felt foolish and disgusted. I tried to talk to him, but that was a disaster. He told me, 'There's no problem. You must be imagining things.'

"Today, we live separate lives under the same roof and I *do* imagine things. I imagine this successful, powerful businessman in the arms of another woman. It's not too difficult to imagine that at all! I live a life of suspicion and distrust, never knowing when I'll find out what I dread finding out, but I'm so sure it is true."

Mary's trust in her husband's commitment is being gradually destroyed by his disinterest. Her wound and her distrust deepen each day as he continues to show indifference toward her. The very nature of erosion obscures its effects. Nothing dramatic happens, just the methodical, often minuscule, movement of sand and silt. Any single snapshot reveals little if any change, but over time, huge amounts of earth are moved.

Over the course of our lives, all of us receive countless messages. While individually insignificant, the negative ones can converge and flow so continuously in our daily experiences that we become denuded of confidence in others and in ourselves. Even though often rendered silently, many of these messages can shape our lives just as inexorably as a slow-moving river. Several messages commonly erode trust. Perhaps you will recognize some of them at work in your own life.

"YOU AREN'T VALUABLE UNLESS YOU ACCOMPLISH CERTAIN GOALS"

Instead of providing a solid, secure base of unconditional acceptance, many families evolve unwritten goals which must be met in order for family members to gain approval. These aspirations may focus on academics or athletics, or they may be rules of "acceptable" behavior, often communicated in absolute terms such as: "We *never* talk that way!" "We *always* do it this way!" "You *ought* to do (be, go, say, etc.) like I do!"

To complicate matters, many families change these rules without notice. What counts as success today may be failure tomorrow. Changing the rules keeps people off-balance, more fearful of condemnation, and more easily manipulated. The designated authority calls the shots and dictates how the game will be played. The person in charge can use a fist or a slightly raised eyebrow or a slightly changed tone of voice to accomplish the same devastating effect.

My daughter spent the night with one of her friends about a month ago. As I drove them home from a party the next week, Catherine invited her friend to a sleepover on Saturday night.

"Oh, I could never do that!" the young girl exclaimed instantly.

I wondered what was behind such a quick and conclusive response. Catherine asked why not.

Her friend explained, "My dad told us we could never spend the night with anyone on Saturday nights. He won't allow it."

"I guess he wants to make sure you'll be ready for church the next day," I wondered out loud.

"I guess so," she replied meekly.

The rule had been imposed. The girl's eyes and voice revealed her fear, even though she didn't know why the rule had been imposed.

Some of us grew up with such high expectations that we couldn't possibly succeed. Nothing we did was ever good enough. I could only shake my head in sorrow as I watched how one father recently behaved at a boys' soccer game. He roamed the sidelines screaming at his son, "Come on! Can't you do any better than that?" "Beat him!" "Get around him!" "You had an open shot! What's the matter with you, Son?" and a host of other loud condemnations.

Sometime during the first half, the boy scored a goal. As he ran back upfield receiving the congratulations of his team-mates, the father yelled to him, "Yeah, but you should have kicked it to the left of the goalie, not the right!" I could only surmise what this boy's life at home was like: constant criticism, with nothing he did being good enough.

Some high expectations are communicated by a parent's articulated rules; some are communicated only when a failure elicits condemnation. A spouse, parent, child, or friend may never define what they want in a relationship, but then loudly communicate displeasure in the many forms of anger, self-pity, and withdrawal. And since these expectations remain unspoken, they can be changed on a whim. Shifting expectations create uncertainty, confusion, and fear in others.

As we grow in wisdom and maturity, we can clearly recognize or sense the oppressive control of unrealistic, unclear expectations. We can ask for explanations, negotiate realistic goals, and confront those who use condemnation in order to control us. However, many of us fall short in exercising such perception and strength. We tend to internalize the anger of others and condemn ourselves for failing. We react to their self-pity or withdrawal and expend our energy trying to help them feel better. We erroneously assume that living up to these expectations will make them happy.

Those who trust blindly become trapped in this web very quickly and burn themselves out trying to live up to the expectations of others. Those who are more passive simply avoid those who expect too much. Those who are more aggressive often find themselves embroiled in a power game, butting heads with someone else. Like two rams during mating season, both may be determined to intimidate and dominate the other.

"YOU AREN'T WORTHWHILE UNLESS YOU MEET MY NEEDS"

Some of us have internalized a slightly different message. We learned that our own needs don't matter, that our role is to make others happy, successful, and good.

A young child who is learning to be autonomous lacks the capacity to give much, but in some families, even small children are expected to take on adult roles. The child may reverse roles with the parent. After Paul's parents divorced when he was six, he lived with his mother. Desperately in need of help, love, and affirmation, she looked to her son to meet those needs. "Oh, Paul, you're the only one I can trust. You're such a sweet and wonderful boy. What would I do without you?" In effect, this young boy took on the role of husband to his mother.

Thirty years later, Paul explained, "I felt powerful around my mother. She depended on me, and I took care of her. But I didn't realize then that I was being someone to her I should never have been expected to be. I was a little boy with little-boy needs, not a man—not her husband. I lived to meet her needs. I became an extension of her, ready and willing to change my emotions and behavior to please her in every way I could."

Paul continued, "If I'm not in a situation in which I feel powerful and needed, I don't know who I am. I felt such power then, but I feel completely empty and lonely now."

If we are in a family or relationship where significant needs exist, where these needs are not addressed appropriately and where our own needs are neglected, we unconsciously try to find some way—any way—to have our own needs for attention and appreciation met. Meeting the needs of others provides an obvious solution. It makes us feel worthwhile.

When someone expresses a need, many of us jump in, ready to rescue. The needy person sometimes demands to be "fixed" and uses self-pity, anger, or appreciation to elicit the desired response. But the fixers can also be demanding. They can demand to be appreciated for their efforts to help someone in need. Of course people who offer help don't want it to look like a demand at all. "I'm just happy to help and serve," fixers might say. Nonetheless, they trust the needy person to be thankful for their efforts, and to give them the appreciation, love, and acceptance which they crave.

Some people would *like* to help so they can feel appreciated, but they've given up. Perhaps they've tried, failed, and experienced the sting of rejection too often. Perhaps they feel worn out. Perhaps they lack enough self-confidence to even try. They doubt their efforts would be effective, but even if they were, they lack the certainty of being rewarded. The slow erosion of trust has undermined their capacity for reaching out to someone in need.

More aggressive people have also given up on trust relationships. They only want to be "one up." Needy people give them that opportunity. In their strength, fixers may despise a needy person's weakness, but welcome the opportunity to show how indispensable they are.

Wisdom can enable us to discern if someone is using their neediness to control us. We can learn to freely say yes when God directs us to help and no when he doesn't. When we don't base our self-confidence on the appreciation of others, we find ourselves less vulnerable to the manipulation of the professionally helpless.

"YOU AREN'T COMPETENT TO MAKE YOUR OWN DECISIONS"

While too little attention leaves children feeling abandoned, too much attention and direction robs a child of self-respect and self-confidence. A friend of mine quips that his mother must not have thought that his brain was standard equipment. He says, "She told me absolutely everything to say, do, be, and go. Later she told me how to vote, how to cook, which girl to date, what to say to her.... It was ridiculous!" My friend laughed at the absurdity of his story, but he wasn't kidding.

I asked him, "How did that kind of attention affect you?"

"The best way to describe it," he told me, "is that for every decision I have made for the past forty-seven years—even little ones like which restaurant to go to or which movie to see—I would instantly see my mother's face, and I'd think, *What would Mom want me to do?* Oh, it wasn't that clearly stated. It was just that she was there making sure I did the 'right thing,' which was what she wanted me to do. It's made me have no confidence in my own ability to make a decision without checking it out with her—or her ghost!—first."

Sometimes we can go overboard in giving attention and praise to children. About a year ago, my son was struggling with his fourth-grade math. When he brought home a paper with a good grade, I'd tell him, "That's great, Son! I'm really proud of you!"

After two or three of these incidents, Taylor looked at me with one of those all-knowing, fourth-grade looks and said, "Dad, it's not that big of a deal, so would you... uh... kind of... ah..."

"Cool it?"

"Yeah." And to be sure he didn't hurt my feelings too much, he added, "If you don't mind."

As children mature, parents need to give them increased responsibility for their own choices and behavior (within expanding limits, of course). If denied the opportunities to succeed and fail, their lives will be neater and more manageable in the short run, but they will fail to develop some of the character qualities needed to be emotionally and relationally healthy adults.

As adults, we can still find ourselves in situations where we hear this message about incompetence. Charlie told me, "I'd worked for this company for three years. I'd done well, gotten a raise every year, good performance reviews, the whole bit. My boss needed some research for an important proposal he was to submit, and he asked me to get him some information. I worked really hard and wrote the report for him. When he presented the proposal at a big sales meeting, somebody asked about one of the projected sales figures. He answered confidently, then more people realized the figures were wrong. I had misplaced the decimal in an earlier computation. The whole thing was wrong! My boss was embarrassed and angry!

"That was six months ago but my boss hasn't forgotten it. Every time he asks me to do something, he asks me a million questions to be sure I won't mess up again. 'Remember this...,' 'Don't forget to...,' 'You'd better...,' 'Go over it one more time to be sure.'"

"OK, I made a mistake. One lousy mistake! I guess I'm not trustworthy anymore."

When we're treated in a similar fashion, we tend to respond in predictable ways: we either try harder to prove ourselves; or we give up and quit trying; or we alternate between the two.

Occasionally, we encounter new and difficult circumstances. We need help. But sometimes that help saps our sense of confidence instead of strengthening it. A woman in her fifties was suddenly widowed when her husband died from a heart attack on a business trip. The flood of shock and grief was compounded by her new responsibilities to handle the family finances, her husband's business interests, and seemingly countless other details which seemed to multiply with each passing day.

She asked her son and some of her friends for help, but she became confused and frustrated by their plentiful advice. Her learning curve was too steep. "I can't do anything right," she lamented. This lovely, energetic—if somewhat overprotected—woman had lost her strength and confidence.

"DON'T BOTHER ME"

"I don't have time for you." "Hurry up! I've got more important things to do than listen to you." "Don't bother me! I'm too busy doing something important." These messages powerfully communicate that we aren't valued. And we don't trust those who don't value us because they don't feel safe.

All of us have been known to use nonverbal messages to communicate disinterest—or worse. Someone may come into our work area to ask a question, but we keep on writing a report. "Go ahead, I'm listening," we might say, but our gestures and lack of eye contact speak louder than our verbal assurances. Other times we may look at our watches, nervously tap our fingers, or mutter quick answers. Such actions say just as loudly, "Don't bother me!"

The closeness of family life provides ample opportunity for messages of disinterest. Parents may struggle just to handle their own problems. They may be so wrapped up in their own emotional wounds that they don't have any energy left for anyone else. Perhaps their strongest values center on acquiring money, status, or possessions instead of caring for their children. Older siblings often express boredom or disdain for younger children's desires and needs. Extenuating circumstances like death, disease, divorce, or duty may place a strain on every member of the family.

Jane's father worked seventy hours a week as a business executive. As soon as he got home, he turned on the TV and read the newspaper. On Saturdays, he worked around the house—by himself—and on Sundays, he played golf. He managed to communicate loud and clear, "Your needs aren't important." Then as if to rub salt into his daughter's wounds, he even added, "And you really don't belong here."

A few times, Jane had tried to pursue her father. "Can I help you paint this room, Daddy?" "Would you like to look at this movie with me?" "What do you think of my new dress, Dad?"

Sometimes her dad ignored her, but more often he reacted in anger, "Can't you see I'm busy? Go and find something constructive to do!"

This man made a good salary and enjoyed a high level of prestige in the community. Many people sought his advice. He had time for everyone and everything, except his family.

When she was a senior in high school, Jane trusted Christ to be her Savior. She enjoyed the warmth and encouragement of her new Christian friends, and she felt very close to God. After a year or so, however, her relationship with God began to grow cold and distant. It soon became a reflection of her relationship with her father. She didn't want to bother God: he might get angry with her.

"I LOVE YOU... GO AWAY"

No one can communicate unconditional love 100 percent of the time. No matter how hard we try, we all send mixed messages. One minute we express our affection to a child or appreciation to a neighbor or co-worker, but then turn right around and apply an eraser. We may issue a very angry message like "You'd better not do that or you'll be sorry!" or a more subtle threat to withdraw our love when someone breaks the rules of acceptable behavior.

A child may bring home a report card with all A's and beam when the father says, "I'm so proud of you!" But coupled with the praise, the child receives constant pushes to excel, often delivered in stern tones of warning: "You'll never get into a good college if you don't study." "I won't be happy if I see one more B in algebra this year." "Second in your class again? You can do better than that, can't you?" "How did Rachel Johnson do in English? Did you get a better grade?"

These comments and questions may seem harmless, but the tone of voice, the praise for excellence, and the lack of tolerance for failure create fear—even though an occasional affirmation is spoken.

A wife may crave the nearness and warmth of intimacy with her husband, but she fears being hurt. She may communicate in classic approach/avoidance: "I love you, darling. You mean so much to me." But as he responds, her defenses rise. She feels threatened, afraid of what her husband might do with tender, personal information. She reacts instinctively to protect herself. "Don't touch me! What do you think you're doing?" Her husband is left confused, hurt, and angry. His wife's desire for intimacy was overshadowed by her distrust. And his trust in her was shaken by her mixed message and sudden, violent reaction.

The pastor of a church may speak eloquently and often of the love of Jesus, but a new member who visits the church office may observe something quite different. The free-flowing gossip negates the message of grace this woman heard on

Sunday morning. Fear and doubt crowd out her faith. When she chooses not to participate in talking about certain members of the church, the raised eyebrows signify that she will be the next target—as soon as she walks out of the room.

Mixed messages take on an especially destructive and manipulative character if they are frequent and if no opportunity is given to talk about the recipient's feelings and perceptions. Mixed messages find their power in an intense tandem of motivations: the desire to be loved and the fear of rejection. These potent forces can make us feel like puppets, eager to do whatever it takes to please. By mixing rewards and punishments, someone can keep us off balance.

STILL HEARING THE SAME MESSAGES

All of these messages are internalized most quickly and profoundly during childhood. Many years later, however, many of us still hear those messages from our friends, spouse, boss, pastor, and anyone else in our lives.

In fact, we may hear those devaluing words even when they aren't meant or spoken by others. We have come to expect them. We trust them to be true. They have become the basis of our identity. They undergird our thought patterns, beliefs, and perceptions about life. And once these messages have eroded our trust and our self-confidence, we are more susceptible to being hurt once again.

Our own errant actions can end up communicating to others in the same ways which have slowly scarred us. Though we may despise the messages we've received, we can easily become transmitters of those same hurtful, condemning, manipulative words. We speak these messages because that's the only thing we've heard, the only model we've been given to follow. And they work. People respond to us the same way we've responded to others: out of the need for affection and the fear of condemnation.

Erosion implies a slow, steady, but powerful process. The

ebbing of our trust occurs because we don't realize what's happening. We make no effort to stop it because we can't see the effects. If we saw these countless, damaging messages for what they are, we could take action, arrest the flow, and build an emotional dike. But we lack the perception to see it, and so we don't take action. We may know something is wrong, but we assume we just need to try even harder, trust (untrustworthy) people a little more, hide more effectively, or take charge of others so they can't hurt us.

Because erosion of trust occurs so slowly, we seldom realize its full impact. We usually minimize the damage ("It wasn't so bad"), excuse the message-bearer ("She couldn't help it"), or deny the whole thing ("I don't know what you're talking about"). Before we examine the various types of trust in greater detail, use the following questions to more clearly perceive how trust has eroded in your own life.

❖ ❖ ❖

Take Time to Reflect

1. Describe who may have communicated eroding messages to you:

   - You aren't valuable unless you accomplish certain goals.
   - You aren't worthwhile unless you meet my needs.
   - You aren't competent to make your own decisions.
   - Don't bother me!
   - I love you. Go away.

2. How did you respond to each of these messages?

3. In what situations or relationships do you find yourself minimizing, excusing, or denying hurts in your life?

PART TWO

❖ ❖ ❖

The Twists and Turns of Trust

5

Perceiving Is Believing

BETWEEN MY SOPHOMORE AND JUNIOR YEARS in college, my buddy, Alfred, and I wanted to do something more adventurous than spend another summer working as laborers for Daniel's Construction Company.

Our next best option took us to Bountiful, Utah, to work at the Trumball Asphalt Company. My Uncle Curtis had just been promoted and relocated from North Carolina, and Aunt Lucille said they'd be glad to have us. The work at the asphalt plant turned out to be not too dissimilar from what we would have been doing for the construction company. But no matter: we were eighteen hundred miles from home!

After a few weeks on the job, Uncle Curtis told us to burn a pile of broken pallets that had accumulated over the past several months. "Just one thing," he warned us, "we're not really supposed to burn anything around here. It's against some stupid city code or something. So be sure the fire doesn't get too big and control it so it doesn't make much smoke. I don't want to get in trouble with the fire department."

"No problem!" we answered simultaneously.

OK! A challenge! And one that had meaning to the company. With a sense of profound importance, Alfred and I surveyed the aforementioned accumulation of debris (important missions require important-sounding words, you know). We carefully started a small fire at the edge of the pile; our plan was to gradually burn the wood as the fire crept forward.

We soon discovered one little bitty problem with our plan, however: it didn't work! The flames got bigger and higher. We tried to rearrange the wood to slow down the fire, but that only made the flames spread more quickly. The smoke was becoming dark and thick, rising higher and higher.

I looked around frantically and spotted a plastic milk jug full of water over near the shed. "Alfred, grab that jug of water and throw it on the fire! Quick!"

Alfred dropped the board he was wrestling, ran a few steps to get the jug, and in one swift and graceful motion, threw the water onto the fire.

Now we had another little bitty problem: the jug contained raw gas, a byproduct of refining oil into asphalt!

You don't have to be a rocket scientist to figure out the next scene. Within a few seconds, every employee of the Trumball Asphalt Company came running to see the conflagration. I still remember Uncle Curtis looking up at the enormous billows of black and gray smoke, with the blaring fire trucks turning in at the gate behind him. That vivid image is, shall we say, burned into my memory.

That experience taught me a lesson on the importance of perception. My insight regarding the "water jug" proved to be miscalculated. My recognition of Uncle Curtis's mood for the next several days turned out to be fairly accurate, however. One out of two isn't bad, is it?

THE VOLATILITY OF PERCEPTIONS

None of us lives by reality; we live by our *perception* of reality. Perceptions are never formed in a vacuum. Events and relationships combine to influence how we view circumstances. The closer and more long-term a relationship we have with someone, the more effect that person's attitudes and actions will have on our worldview.

Others influence our preferences: we love Italian food, we

despise board games, we like to wear green, we hate squatty cars. Others mold our values: whether we are racist or tolerant, pro-choice or anti-abortion, conniving or honorable. And they shape our deepest drives: our hopes and fears, optimism or bleak outlook, emotional strength or escapism.

Nowhere is the potential for shaping our perceptions greater than in the family. But we shouldn't make the mistake of thinking that children will be "just like" their parents. Some are. Some are in some ways but not in others. Others vehemently react *against* what their parents believe and value, wanting to be just the opposite. Even in their reaction, however, these rebels reflect the shaping process of the family.

As a relatively closed system which spans years, the family unit is a universe unto itself where perceptions of reality are created and reinforced without much challenge. The beliefs and values of a family may strike objective observers as distorted while seeming logical to family members. They believe the "truth" taught to them within the family system.

Examples can be seen walking into the offices of counselors and pastors every day. Men, women, and children reveal long-buried stories of abandonment, abuse, and manipulation. Questions such as, "Did you know it didn't have to be that way?" or "What would it feel like to be loved and valued?" draw a look of confusion.

"What do you mean?" one woman asked me.

"I mean you have worth and value because you are made in the image of God. And you can have your own identity and make your own choices instead of always doing what others want you to do."

Like most of us, this lady needed a few weeks for the truth to sink in. "But I always thought my family was normal. You mean, not everybody feels the way I do?"

REALITY CHECKS

Why do we so often reach faulty conclusions? Why do we misjudge people or situations based on poor perception? There are many possible answers, but two suggest themselves immediately: first, we have nothing with which to compare our own sense of reality; second, we are rewarded for upholding the family's view of reality and punished for challenging it.

We need "reality checks," usually from outside sources, to help us gain perspective on our feelings and behaviors—and on the feelings and behaviors of others. Without this feedback we usually stay locked in the system. We continue to respond to the wide range of rewards and punishments which may be used by that family structure: physical (e.g., hugs, beatings); material (e.g., food, toys, withholding of these); verbal (e.g., praise, change in tone of voice, criticism); nonverbal (e.g., smiles, scowls, raised eyebrows); time (e.g., attention, neglect); or most likely, some combination of these.

In a closed system without objective input, rewards and punishments are extremely effective in controlling us. As we saw in the previous chapters, they are also effective at destroying trust. When our perceptions are inaccurate, we will gravitate to the extremes of either trusting untrustworthy people or trusting no one at all.

If we have grown up in a skewed system, how can we gain accurate perceptions? Apart from divine infusion, we learn by watching wise people and from experience. Many of us, however, haven't been around wise people very often. The modeling we saw tended to be more reactionary than patient. We didn't feel safe enough for trial and error: our errors brought too much condemnation and guilt. Instead of encouragement for our successes and forgiveness for our failures, we often received quick fixes or no help at all.

Without any encouragement to hold these complexities in tension, we feel threatened. Our craving for safety makes us want to escape. We may desperately want to believe that someone is safe, so we deny reality. We minimize and excuse their untrustworthy behavior. "It wasn't that bad." "She couldn't help it," we say.

Or we repress a painful event as if it never happened at all.

Magically thinking they'll come through for us, we decide to trust untrustworthy people, even if their track record overwhelmingly points in the opposite direction. Perhaps we subconsciously believe that if we trust them, they are then obligated to treat us properly. "I proved myself to them," we may think, "so they have to prove themselves to me."

Others who aren't foolish enough to trust someone undeserving of trust may instead fall into hopelessness. We may give up on finding a relationship of respect, love, and trust. We either withdraw from others, or we seek to dominate them. Both methods are designed to control their access to us.

WHAT CAUSES SKEWED SIGHT?

The degree to which perception and trust become distorted hinges on several factors.

The intensity of the events. Some of us experienced shattering blows such as sexual or physical abuse, car wrecks or other accidents, or perhaps military combat. Those of us who were emotionally or physically abandoned often feel an intense, amorphous emptiness.

Some of us have been sheltered from as much hurt as possible by well-meaning parents or spouses. Intended to protect us, this shielding prevents us from going through experiences which can impart wisdom and strength of character. Overprotection actually proves detrimental to the development of perception.

We also find that through the normal ups and downs—the very trials and joys of life—we learn to trust wisely as our perception of people, events, and ourselves becomes clearer. We realize that we have skills and abilities to meet life's challenges, which develops inner strength. If all goes well, we also recognize our sinfulness and inadequacies, true wisdom which leads us to acknowledge our genuine need for God.

Duration and frequency. Our wounds may have been inflicted over a short period of time or over a period of years.
Painful events may have occurred only once; they may have
occurred daily or hourly.

Age. Typically, the earlier we experience trauma and stress, the
more damage results because we are more psychologically vulnerable and have fewer coping skills. Someone from a relatively
healthy, stable home environment who has learned to be honest about feelings and to communicate with others can usually
handle emotional pain more effectively than fragile or heavily
defended people. Also, those who have had the opportunity
and time to develop their perceptive abilities will be less likely
to be severely wounded in relationships. They are more likely
to determine which risks are wise and which are foolish.

Personality. Determining a person's true personality is often
difficult. Personality tests and inventories may reveal only the
composite of defense mechanisms the person has developed. A
person's true personality may be hidden from the test. Indeed,
it may be stunted and buried, undetectable by any instrument.
Some tests, however, can reveal certain *tendencies* in motivation, relationship needs, communication styles, conflict resolution, intensity, and other components of our sense of identity
and how we relate to other people and tasks.

Studying the roles we play in our families—and subse-
quently, in other relationships as well—provides a helpful
corollary to personality inventories. Many professionals have
described these roles or masks in various ways, such as enabler,
hero, mascot, scapegoat, lost child, nice guy/girl, and tough
guy/girl.

There is a relationship between our family roles and our
capacity to trust. The enabler and the hero tend to blindly
trust; the lost child and the nice guy/girl tend to passively distrust; and the tough guy/girl typically employs aggressive distrust. The mascot may develop either blind trust or passive

distrust. Scapegoats follow a more complicated pattern. They may begin by blindly trusting, and then turn to passive distrust in the early stages of being blamed for the family's problems. In their anger, scapegoats may then try to intimidate others through aggressive distrust.

Emotional and physical health. Our emotional and physical health at the time we experience trauma significantly affects how we interpret the events. Those who are depressed tend to see painful events as devastating and hopeless. Similarly, those with physical difficulties—as chronic and debilitating as paralysis or as mild and temporary as a cold—often interpret events through dark-colored glasses.

These factors affect our ability to perceive reality and our capacity to trust ourselves and others. The powerfully destructive combination of an unsafe environment, our inability to recognize the danger, and the rewards and punishments which keep us locked into the system can drive us to extremes. We trust blindly or not at all. How extreme we are is a function of the factors we just examined. Some of us may fall on middle ground.

AN INTRICATE MOSAIC

In the next few chapters, we will examine the three trust styles in more detail, but I wanted to insert a note of caution first. Very few of us fit into only one category. For example, you may exhibit passive distrust in certain kinds of relationships, or that may be your dominant style, but you may respond very differently in other relationships. Let's examine some of the situations that determine our trust/relational patterns.

Finding our place in the pecking order. We may respond differently to those in authority over us than we do to those under us. We may blindly trust or passively not trust those above us because we feel intimidated by their perceived power. On the other hand, we may aggressively dominate someone under our authority. For instance, a wife may meekly submit (passive distrust) to her powerful, dominating husband, but she may be quite forceful in her relationship with her children. Or middle managers may be driven to please a boss they idolize (blind trust), but treat subordinates harshly as a way to stimulate productivity.

Some of us exhibit the opposite pattern. We behave aggressively toward those above us on the pecking order and passively toward those under us. Anger may propel us to react to the person in charge. We refuse to be controlled, even by authority figures who genuinely care for us. Our attitude says, "I'm not going to take anything from you!" We demand to be appreciated, but our self-defeating behavior only creates more tension and suspicion.

Passivity toward those under us may be a result of having spent our emotional energies fighting with authority figures. Or we may simply disdain those under us, deeming them to be unworthy of our time. Of course, some of us feel aggressive and angry toward those above *and* beneath us. We may be so defiant that we won't let anybody control us.

Avoiding or creating conflict. Many of us avoid dealing with conflict, but when a crisis occurs, our adrenaline kicks in. We begin issuing orders and making things happen. Perhaps a husband comes home drunk, a wife has a car accident, a child gets into serious trouble at school, or a parent dies suddenly—some incident serious enough to overcome our normal passivity. Conversely, more aggressive people who seem quite comfortable inducing stress in others' lives may suddenly wilt in a crisis. They become indecisive and inactive, passively looking around for somebody to tell them what to do.

Hanging on to memories. Particularly stressful events become imprinted on our memories and color our thinking and behavior for years to come.

Let me tell you a story which illustrates this. Over Christmas break one year when I was in college, I was asked to deliver presents to family friends. After several stops, I pulled down a long driveway, gathered up an armload of presents, and started walking toward the front door. Only a few steps later I heard a loud bark and saw a huge, gray dog streaking around the far corner of the house. It was an enormous German shepherd, and he was not happy that I was on his turf!

In a heartbeat—I thought it would be my last!—this ferocious animal was only a few feet from me. As he jumped and lunged at my throat, I turned. He bit through four layers of clothes. When he let go and dropped to the ground, I instinctively stuck my foot in his mouth. My tennis shoes were expendable; my throat was not. The German shepherd tore into that shoe like a buzz saw, shaking his head to tear flesh from bone, but shredding only rubber instead. A petite, twelve-year-old girl who had heard the barking and growling came out of the house and beat the dog until he let go.

"We just got back from a trip and Duke was caged the whole time. I guess it made him a little upset," she said sheepishly. "Are you OK?"

"Uh, yeah," I said articulately. (After all, I had just escaped having my head literally bitten off by a cross between a wolf and a pickup truck! I wanted to count my body parts and see if any teeth were still implanted in my back or foot before I said too much.) "Sure, no problem.... Uh... here are presents for your family." Then I jumped into the car and got out of Dodge!

That was years ago. Today, we have some big dogs in our neighborhood. Occasionally one of these unleashed monsters prowls around while Joyce and I are out walking. When I see one, my memory bank instantly flashes the images of that German shepherd coming at me at Mach Six. Being a he-man, macho type, I quickly jump behind Joyce—if my muscles don't freeze first. My fear calms down only a little bit when Joyce says, "Oh, look, he's a nice dog. He won't hurt us."

"Well... you never know," I hem and haw. People tell me

wonderful stories about noble, loving, affectionate German shepherds. Sorry, I don't buy it. They're bloodthirsty killers. Always have been. Always will be. I don't trust 'em.

Feeling a heightened sense of danger. The more we perceive ourselves to be threatened, the more extreme the measures we take to protect ourselves from further hurt. Also, the more extreme the trust issues. Some of us feel relatively safe; our minor problems of mistrust have limited consequences. For others of us, however, our perception is severely stunted by our heightened sense of danger. We lack any semblance of objectivity regarding the trustworthiness of others. We then feel forced to use stronger measures to control people, both to keep them from hurting us and to win some sense of approval from them.

Continuing to change and grow. Our perceptive skills are never static. Events and relationships can contribute—positively or negatively—to our ability to perceive clearly and to our capacity for trust. Additional trauma and continued exposure to eroding influences can drive us farther to the extremities of mistrust. Healing, honest, nurturing relationships, however, offer us objectivity, hope, and growth.

As we discussed in chapter two, we all enter life with God-given, instinctive trust. The climb toward perceptive trust begins as our basic needs for nurture, food, and warmth are validated. The climb continues through the years of developing autonomy—trust in our ability to make our own decisions—and identity.

Our perceptions have been formed by many powerful influences. Like bricks cemented into the wall of our relationships and experiences, our views can become firmly established. But they can change. No matter how delightful or ugly the influences have been, no matter how accurate or false our perception of reality may be, we can learn to see the truth and trust perceptively.

The first step in resolving a problem is to define and under-

stand the issues fully. In the next few chapters, we will first analyze the three faulty types of trust, and then examine healthy,
mature, wise trust. A friend of mine said, "You never help
yourself by fooling yourself." The next chapters are designed
to give you insight so you can make wiser choices, and perhaps,
stop fooling yourself.

❖ ❖ ❖

Take Time to Reflect

1. Describe how each of these factors has influenced your ability to perceive accurately:

   • the intensity of events

   • duration and frequency

   • age

   • personality

   • emotional and physical health

2. Do any of the following styles characterize the ways in which
   you typically respond to difficulties? If so, describe how.

   • finding your place in the pecking order

   • avoiding or creating conflict

   • hanging on to memories

   • feeling a heightened sense of danger

6

Don't Take Any Wooden Nickels

"WHEN I GREW UP, your grandmother almost smothered me with directions," Charlie told his children as they listened intently to every word. "Grandma told me, 'Good going, Charlie!' every time I did something right. And she let me know about every time I did something wrong, too—in detail!"

My friend's children laughed—a little. Having spent time with Grandma, they too had been the recipients of her play-by-play, color commentary and keen analysis of everything they said or did.

"Your grandmother told me everything. She told me how to brush my teeth, when to go to the bathroom, which friends to have, where to play, when to play, what to play, how to play, how to study, how to relate to adults, how to relate to friends." Charlie paused a moment as this litany sank into his own mind, as well as the children's. Then he summarized, "Your grandmother told me everything to know, be, say, and do!"

Nine-year-old James had a look of profound reflection on his face. Then wisdom slowly blossomed. "So when you were a kid," James paused for dramatic effect, "your mother was your brain."

Anyone can employ blind trust as a way of coping with the untrustworthiness of others. However, empirical evidence and reason both suggest that those who have been smothered by too much attention, direction, and criticism show a greater propensity toward blind trust.

Smothering parents convey the message, "You aren't capable of making your own decisions. You have to trust me to run your life." Rewards for compliance along with punishment for "rebellion" (attempting to move toward healthy autonomy) cement the self-perception of those who trust blindly: "I can't make my own decisions. I have to trust others to know what's best for me."

Like Charlie, people who trust blindly let others function as their brains. Their unsafe environment makes them desperately want to feel secure. They subconsciously block out threats to their security. Pleasing others enough to win their approval becomes the chief means of achieving the coveted goal: safety.

In their eagerness to please, however, those who trust without question are easily manipulated. A host of verbal and nonverbal devices can be used to "push someone's buttons," such as anger, self-pity, withdrawal, praise, condemnation, guilt, or thanks. Individuals who trust blindly wear large buttons which are easily pushed! Almost any type of communicator can get them to jump!

After Charlie described how his identity was wrapped up in his mother's, I asked him, "Did you become passive in that relationship or did you actively try to please her?"

"Passive?" Charlie chuckled. "Well, maybe in some ways, but my overwhelming and continuous goal was to try to please her in every way I could. If Mom was unhappy, it was up to me to make her happy. I was so driven to please her that I tried really hard to anticipate her every need before she could say she had it. In fact, if my mother said she needed something, I was too late. I had failed. Even though I tried everything to make her happy, I had failed because I didn't read her mind. Yeah, I guess you could say I actively tried to please her!"

ACTIVELY PLEASING OTHERS

In their desperation to please people and win their approval, those who trust without question develop finely tuned antennae. They are perceptive about what pleases or displeases other people, but not about the hurt, anger, and manipulation in their own lives. They are blind to all that.

One woman told me, "I've learned to read the slightest change in the voice inflection of others to see if their comment tells me I've said or done the right thing. I discern the faintest lift of an eyebrow or the most subtle smile or frown. I am constantly analyzing people's responses, like a radar looking for anything suspicious, anything that might threaten, or anything that might bring comfort and affirmation. I am tremendously perceptive... except when it comes to me, my needs, how others manipulate me, and how I get locked into pleasing people instead of being myself."

In order to keep their fragile world together, those who trust blindly idealize their parents, and later other authorities such as spouse, boss, pastor, and God. In their eyes, such authority figures are always good and right, and always have the person's best interests at heart. This "white" view of authority makes them feel safe, even though it may be based on unrealistic perceptions and expectations.

Of course, the flip side is reserved for those who try to point out the inconsistencies, inappropriate behavior, or harmful motives of these cherished, idealized authorities. This "black" view is directed toward those who've been trusted and found lacking. These scoundrels don't just have a few flaws; they've fallen far from their lofty pedestals.

The more powerful the relationship, the more blindly trusting souls need to keep that person on the pedestal at all costs. Parents and God typically stay on top as long as possible because their fall would devastate the person's fragile worldview.

Those who practice blind trust generally try to avoid conflict by pleasing others so much that friction never happens. When conflict can't be avoided, their next best option is to excuse the offender: "She couldn't help it." "He didn't really mean what he said." Or to minimize the offense: "It didn't affect me. I can take it." "That wasn't so bad."

As types of denial, excusing and minimizing shield those who blindly trust from confronting the realization that they aren't safe. They may be willing to recognize that people around them have done wrong, are alcoholic, are irresponsible, and have hurt them, but they always twist the facts to soften the brutal truth.

Those who actively seek to please others and avoid conflict believe whatever anyone tells them. They are gullible. People who trust blindly must learn to think more critically, to be more cautious, and to ask a second and third question about a person or a situation.

Being gullible can get you into a lot of trouble. Before you read the following story, I want you to know that I did not want to include it in this book. But Joyce has prodded, encouraged, cajoled, and begged me to. It makes her laugh every time she hears it. So against my better judgment, I'm going to throw my reputation to the wind and tell you one of my own "gullible's travels."

Last September, Taylor wanted to play on a soccer team. He brought a note home from school about the registration date, cost, and other information. We were specifically instructed to bring a copy of his birth certificate as proof of age. The Saturday of registration rolled around. "Joyce, I'm going to take Taylor to sign up for a soccer team. Do you have his birth certificate?"

She replied, "I've looked all over for it. I know it's here somewhere, but I just can't find it. Here, take Taylor's baby book. It has his birth announcement in it."

"But we need the certificate," I insisted. "We have to find it before we go."

"I'm sure the baby book will be just fine."

"Honey," I said incredulously, "I don't think the book will work."

"Oh, yeah, it'll be fine," my wife insisted. "They can look at his birth announcement and see his date of birth. That's all they want anyway. Take it up there. You'll see. I bet lots of people couldn't find their child's birth certificate."

Telling myself that we were running late, and that if Joyce couldn't find the certificate I wouldn't either, I took the baby book.

"OK, Taylor, let's go." We hopped in the car and drove over to the Lutheran church where the registration was being conducted.

I walked in the door and soon spotted the table labeled: Boys, ten to eleven years old, M-Z. "That's the one over there, Son. Let's go." With Taylor in tow, I strode in that direction.

The man sitting behind the table said, "I need to see the boy's birth certificate."

I took the ten-by-twelve baby book with the big butterfly on the cover from under my arm. I opened it to Taylor's birth announcement and said, "I don't have the certificate, but this announcement will do."

At that instant, a rush of revelation told me, "I am a fool!" As I looked into the man's face, his expression confirmed, "You ARE a fool!"

"But, I, uh, I guess this won't do, will it?" I quickly closed the book, stuffed it under my arm (I couldn't make it vanish completely as I hoped!), and said tersely, "Come on, Son."

When we got back home, something in my expression told Joyce what had happened. Without a word, she imagined the scene at the registration table with her he-man husband offering another grown man a look at a big book with a butterfly on the cover. Then she burst into peals of laughter—for the first of many times.

Perhaps I should have trusted my instincts. Perhaps I should have waited until we found Taylor's birth certificate. Perhaps next time I'll analyze Joyce's suggestions more carefully. Perhaps I should change my name and move to another town. (Now, if you don't mind, please tear these pages out of your book and throw them away. I have my reputation to protect, you know.)

ELUSIVE POWER

As we saw in chapter two, autonomy involves the confidence to make our own decisions without self-doubt or self-contempt. If we never develop a sense of autonomy, we feel the need to have others make decisions for us.

Rachel described it this way: "All my life I've felt like I had the ghost of my dad hovering over me. Every decision I made, I'd subconsciously wonder, *What do I need to do to please Dad? What would he want me to do?* But I never realized I was so dominated by him until I got into my group and listened to other people tell how their decisions are shaped by others. The sick thing is, I'm forty-five years old and my father has been dead for years! Why in the world do I let him keep determining the course of my life?"

The apparent impetus for such behavior is *hope*, hope of winning love and acceptance. Linda described her intense motivation: "I wanted to please my parents and my brother so badly! My mom was devastated by her father's death and by her third miscarriage when I was seven. After that, I guess Dad couldn't stand the strain, so he was away a lot on business trips. I felt lonely. I felt that if I could just make Mom happy again, everything would be OK! Later I realized that 'the family being OK' meant that I would be OK. You know, safe."

While the surface motivation may be the hope of being loved and safe, the underlying stimulus is fear: the fear of being hurt again, the fear of being abandoned, the fear of being a nobody. This lethal combination of false hope and true fear keeps many people in denial, driven to please others.

Trapped in this dual motivation, individuals who trust blindly often analyze everything they say and do—and everything other people say and do to them—in an effort to find something safe. Unfortunately, their search usually proves futile. It frequently leads to more shame because they focus more on what they "should have said," "ought to have done," or "what Fran really meant when she said...."

In fact, shame itself becomes another facet of the underlying motivation of someone who is enmeshed in these patterns. While a sense of worthlessness drives some people to passivity, it tends to energize and focus those who trust blindly to prove their value to others. Again, they hope that pleasing people and fixing their problems will earn some appreciation and recognition. They feel, *I am a worthless person, but I can prove I am somebody by making others happy.*

One lady told me, "The only time I feel good about myself is when I'm helping others. When they appreciate it, I feel strong. In fact, I feel indispensable! They needed me and I came through!"

That aura of power, however, quickly fades. People who trust blindly surrender their power to others. If others appreciate their efforts, then the person feels strong. If not, an overly trusting person feels empty, guilty, and crushed. The power or locus of control resides not within the individual, but with others who are allowed to determine how he or she thinks, feels, and acts.

TRUST AS MANIPULATION

A friend of mine described a business deal he had with a close friend. Roy related, "When I first got into this deal, I thought: Harold is a creative guy with lots of good ideas about making money. But you know something strange? He never seems to put it all together. Something always happens to him... bad luck, I guess. I felt sorry for him, and I thought I could help him. He gave me a great business plan for a real estate development, so I invested the start-up money. Harold assured me I'd make that and a lot more in only a few months.

"Well, we got started and everybody was very enthusiastic. He gave me glowing reports about progress on the roads, water, and all the other parts of the development. After a few months, though, Harold called and said he needed some more money. 'A temporary cash flow problem,' he said. I sent him a check.

"More glowing reports. Then another call for more money. I asked a few questions, but he seemed irritated by my asking them. Harold asked, 'Don't you trust me?'

"Hey, I didn't want to discourage the guy. 'Yes, of course I do. No problem.'

"A few more months, another call for some money. This time, I didn't ask any questions—just a mumbled request that Harold be sure he knows where the money's going. He knew!

"After the first of the year I needed to get my taxes filed so I asked Harold for a K-1 statement. He assured me the CPA was working on it. Seven calls later, no K-1. I guess she was a little slow! Finally, I called the CPA myself. She said, 'Do you know what's going on with Harold and the money?' My heart sank—and I had a feeling my wallet was going to do the same thing.

"I went in to see the CPA. She showed me the accounting report. Harold had sold a lot of the property, but he had taken all the money and left me with the debt!

"I'm thinking about legal action. I'm actually thinking about murder! But I'm not sure who deserves it: him or me."

Why would a mature, bright adult like Roy be so foolish to trust someone like Harold, and *keep* trusting him when all the warning signals were brightly flashing?

As we talked, Roy explained how he had always liked Harold and wanted their friendship to grow. The business deal offered a way to show his support and solidify their relationship. They would be closer than ever. Even when he had every reason to question Harold's trustworthiness, Roy chose to continue to have faith in him. The risk of creating conflict deterred Roy from asking the hard questions. The risk of losing a friend hindered him from honest confrontation and remedial action.

A psychologist friend offered his assessment of blind trust: "Blind trust is manipulative. Its goal is to get other people to treat us well." That appraisal may seem harsh, but it's true. The subconscious reasoning behind blind trust is, *I'm trusting you to be nice to me, so please don't hurt me.* In that case, we may be trusting someone to do what he or she will not or cannot do.

I often detect another subconscious motivation behind blind trust: "I'm doing all this to help you, to please you, and to fix your problems. I'm giving my life for you! So I deserve for you to treat me well, meet my needs, and make me happy." These individuals expect (demand!) that others balance the scale and do as much for them as they've been doing.

People who employ blind trust are usually quite skilled socially. They're good at reading gestures, expressions, and tone of voice to discern if others are happy. They can then say the right words or do the right thing to make someone feel better. There is nothing inherently wrong in this ability to please others. At issue here are the motives, not the actions. The same words can be spoken or actions performed to either love openhandedly or to manipulate to gain approval.

In the midst of conflict, blind trust shows its true colors:

- giving in to demands
- internalizing blame
- wilting under pressure
- withdrawing
- using self-pity to get others to care

These devices are primarily designed to win leverage, to earn love, attention, and safety. Those of us who trust without question tend to actively try to gain this leverage, but generally become quite passive in conflict and wilt under the pressure. As the unresolved hurt and anger build, however, we may explode in anger from time to time. If venting our wrath convinces others to give in, we add the expression of anger to our repertoire of manipulative devices. Then we can internalize blame (it's all my fault) and/or externalize blame (the conflict is all your fault).

Blind trust normally leads us to assume the blame and to take responsibility for the unhappiness and inappropriate behavior of others. The sense of shame and unworthiness generally transcends our anger toward others, which is then turned inward to wreak havoc in our emotional and spiritual lives.

GOD, THE GREAT FIXER

A few months ago, I talked to a group about the four kinds of trust. I asked them, "Is it a good thing to blindly trust God?"

"It's always good to trust God completely," stated one person unequivocally.

Another responded with a blend of confusion and anger, "He's trustworthy, isn't he? Why can't we blindly trust him?"

Next came a less confrontational response: "The problem with blind trust is the 'truster,' isn't it? So even though God *is* 100 percent trustworthy, blindly trusting him isn't good."

My question stimulated a more spirited debate than I expected. Perhaps the reason is simple: as I mentioned earlier, we tend to generalize our view of our parents to all authority figures. If our parents loved and protected us, then we usually feel unafraid of authority figures. If our parents were harsh, smothering, or abusive, we will probably believe that others in authority are out to get us, too. If our parents were aloof and neglectful, we will tend to feel isolated from authority.

Those of us who have blindly trusted authority figures usually demand too much of God. We work hard for him and so we expect him to take care of us. Instead of understanding the appropriate blend of God's enablement and our responsibility (for instance, see Phil 2:12 and 2 Cor 6:1), we focus primarily on God's end of the deal. We become passive, expecting him to fix our problems.

Our expectations of God are rooted in the same reasoning we apply to others: "If I trust him, then he has to prove he's trustworthy by meeting my needs." Or, "I'm doing so much for God, I deserve for him to meet my needs. It's only fair." Of course, we are usually oblivious to such thoughts.

What happens when we expect God to provide for us because we trust him and are driven to do things for him? We experience bitter disappointment when God "doesn't come through."

Years ago, I knew a young couple at the University of North Carolina. Both were committed Christians. A member of the wrestling team, the husband looked like the picture of health. We met fairly regularly to talk about the Lord and to pray together.

One day I could see the dejection on their faces as I walked toward them. "We just found out... Bill has cancer." Sarah broke into tears. We sat together for a while, wondering how someone so strong and so robust could be so sick.

A couple of weeks later, we met again. This time, their faces glowed. I wondered what was up. "The Lord has given us a promise," Bill grinned. "We know he's going to heal me."

"It's in Psalm 91," Sarah excitedly added as she turned in her Bible. We read the whole Psalm, then Bill pointed to verses 15 and 16.

He will call upon me, and I will answer him;
I will be with him in trouble;
I will rescue him, and honor him,
With a long life I will satisfy him,
And let him behold my salvation.

"That's the promise," Bill declared solemnly and with deep conviction. "I'm going to be all right."

I saw this couple a few more times in the next month, but then I lost sight of them for a while. Then one day I saw Sarah sitting alone. She looked crushed. I walked up to her as she continued to stare at the floor. In a few moments, she looked up at me. "Bill's dead," Sarah said blankly. "He died two weeks ago." We sat together for a long while with only a few words passing between us. Then, this forlorn wife cried, "Why? Why did God let Bill die? He promised!"

I don't question that God can lead us to trust him for specific answers. He can and he does. But blind trust encourages us to see promises where God doesn't intend them. We sometimes believe that God wants to bail us out of difficult circumstances when he may want to give us strength to go through them. We may feel that our trust somehow guarantees God's response to our needs, and that our activity obliges him to fix our problems.

Blind trust prompts us to believe God for things he has never purposed to do. We think we deserve it, and then when God "fails," we make excuses, we minimize the hurt, and we blame ourselves, still blindly trusting. We continue this sightlessness until we experience a loss so devastating that we can no longer excuse God or minimize his neglect. When this happens, we often move from blind trust to no trust.

❖ ❖ ❖

Take Time to Reflect

Indicate whether or not the following statements are true of the way you usually respond:

yes no I feel guilty when I believe I could have done something to prevent harm from occurring.

yes no I usually go out of my way to please other people.

yes no I feel insecure when I don't feel closely attached to other people.

yes no I'll do practically anything to avoid an argument.

yes no I tend to look for the bright sides of things, no matter how bleak the situation may be.

yes no I actively seek out opportunities in which I can help others.

yes no I am able to see the good in even the most negative individuals.

yes no I probably do more to serve others than I do to serve my own needs.

yes no My feelings are easily hurt when others react negatively to me.

yes no I am willing to take chances to give others an opportunity to prove themselves to me.

yes no People tell me I'm gullible.

yes no I watch others very closely to try to detect any changes or shifts in their emotions.

yes no Even when others have failed me, I tend to give them "one more chance" to prove themselves.

yes no I'm happy only if those I care about are happy.

yes no You could say that my self-esteem is fragile.

yes no I can be fairly easily persuaded by someone who is a good communicator.

yes no I have a tendency to assume blame when things go wrong.

yes no If I have a negative opinion, I generally keep it to myself.

yes no My feelings tend to ride an emotional roller coaster—most of the time.

yes no I am seldom aggressive in my communication with others.

If you circle yes to ten or more of the above items, you have tendencies toward blind trust. Answering the following questions will shed more light on how trust operates in your day-to-day life (or in the life of someone close to you).

1. What "payoff" do you get (or hope to get) from others by trusting blindly?

2. In what ways do you please people as a manipulative behavior?

3. Many people who trust blindly seem to have a strong personality and identity. If this is true of you, what underlying identity problems might you be hiding?

4. How does blind trust strengthen your relationship with God? What are some hindrances?

5. How do you feel and act around other people who trust blindly? Why?

7

Getting Away or Giving In

"MY DAD WAS A WORKAHOLIC," Deborah told me. "He worked about seventy to eighty hours a week in his plumbing business. But really, it wasn't so bad that he was gone all the time because he and Mom fought like crazy when he came home. Maybe that's why he stayed away so much.

"My mother was an angry person. She was mad because Dad wasn't more supportive. She had to raise my three brothers and two sisters and me pretty much by herself. My brothers and sisters fought a lot too. Picked it up from Mom and Dad, I guess. I'm next to the youngest, so I don't remember a time that my whole family wasn't mad at each other."

I asked Deborah, "How did all this tension affect you? How did you try to cope?"

"Every day when I got home from school, I went to my room to read, do homework, play with dolls... anything to be by myself. Summer was especially hard because I didn't have homework as an excuse to go to my room. I'd try to stay by myself as much as I could, then after supper, I'd say I had to go to bed."

"What time was that?"

"Oh, about eight o'clock or so. You know, the sun hadn't even gone down!"

"Did your brothers and sisters give you a hard time about going to bed so early?" I wondered.

"Yeah, they sure did! But their name-calling and laughing at me didn't exactly make me want to be around them any longer!"

We talked some more, and then I asked, "Deborah, do you remember giving in when you got into an argument in order to avoid any more conflict?"

"Do I remember?" she laughed. "I don't have to have too good a memory. I still do it!"

"Why do you think you do that? What does giving in do for you?"

Deborah thought for a long while. "I don't know," she finally said. "I guess letting people have whatever they want lessens the tension. I can't stand conflict, so I try to get it over with as quickly as I can!"

Deborah tried to cope with family stress by becoming invisible. She still lives by the rule, "Don't make waves!" She crawls into her shell like a turtle who feels threatened. Deborah responds to others with passive distrust.

AN EVER-SHRINKING WORLD

People who passively distrust others usually try to be pleasant and positive. They rarely say anything negative about anybody, and they typically are glad to help when asked. They differ from the blind-trust types who don't wait to be asked, who aggressively prove their helpfulness.

One woman told me, "About the only messages I ever got from my mother—and there weren't many—were, 'You're such a nice girl. You don't give me problems like your brother!' That became my goal: to avoid giving Mom any problems."

Rather than trying to achieve safety by winning the approval of others, those who passively distrust either give in or get away. They tend to be more perceptive than the first type. At least they realize problems exist and that certain people are untrustworthy. Their solutions, however, lead not to resolution and health but to continued repression and pain. They realize they aren't safe, so they don't trust.

Similar to those who exercise blind trust, those who practice passive distrust internalize the tension, anger, and hurt around them. They believe they're at fault, that they are essentially bad people. They feel worthless and ashamed, but lack the false hope that others really care about them and will ultimately meet their needs if pleased enough. Their lack of trust leaves them dominated by their fears of being hurt again, of being exposed and ridiculed, of being laughed at, of getting close, and of being abandoned (to name only a few).

Though they may seem independent, those who passively distrust are not autonomous. They are isolated. Their aloneness is full of shame and second-guessing. Fear motivates these individuals to be alone.

Family members often reinforce this loneliness and isolation because passive people don't cause problems and fade into the background. These individuals, sometimes called "lost children," can be forgotten by the rest of the family. One man told me, "My dad would ask everybody for their opinion but me. I guess he didn't think I had one."

June told her fellowship group, "Last summer I went to my parents' home for a few days. While I was there, I looked through some old family photographs. After a while, it dawned on me that I wasn't even in a lot of them! They had taken pictures of the family, but they didn't even consider me a part of it! And the ones I was in, I was partly hidden in the back or looking down or in another direction." This grown woman wept at the realization of her abandonment and emptiness.

Unlike those who trust blindly, people who passively distrust don't become enmeshed. They feel alone. Rather than creating a fragile universe populated by people they feel compelled to please, those who passively distrust create a rigid universe of their own thoughts, excluding—as much as possible—anyone or anything which might threaten them. Many become introspective, analyzing every thought, action, and conversation to detect something good and safe in it. More often than not, their morbid analysis uncovers more threats and instability. They condemn themselves for "being so stupid" or "being such a jerk." They call themselves horrible names, thereby reinforcing their singular shame and self-hatred.

THE POWER TO HIDE

Passive people feel and act powerless. They let others control their environment and decisions. Counselors sometimes make simple and even oblique suggestions such as, "Would you tell your husband what you just told me about how you feel?" Or, "What would happen if you said no to her... made your own decision... stated what you would like in the relationship?"

These elementary questions are usually met with a mixture of shock and fear. Many passive individuals will blurt out, "I can't do that!" As we talk about it more and work out a specific plan of communication, they often feel stronger. Then the frightening reality of confrontation hits home and they wilt.

Passive distrust empowers people to do one thing: to hide. "I can do that!" one lady told me as she laughed and described her decision to leave the room. When they hide behind a paper, close the door, or isolate themselves, passive people feel in control of their lives. But even in hiding, many of them feel the pangs of shame and guilt for making such "selfish" decisions.

"I don't know what's wrong with me," Marianne confided. "The only time I feel good about myself is when I'm alone. But when I'm closing the door, I feel so guilty. I think, I ought to be helping Jim or the kids. I ought to be more personable; I ought to communicate more. I feel so ashamed."

Passive individuals can idolize those who are causing them so much stress, even while they internalize this stress as their fault. This idealization seems odd and out of place among a group of people who tend to be more objective about the stress they experience and the pain they feel. But, if the threat of being hurt again is too real, too apparent, even passive people can convince themselves that someone is really "all good"—at least until the evidence of untrustworthiness accumulates or a traumatic event shatters this perception.

To summarize, a person who passively distrusts feels isolated, lonely, and powerless. These individuals live in fear and try to find safety by getting away or giving in.

SUBTLE CONTROL

"Controlling others? What are you talking about? Passive people don't control anybody!" As I began to talk about the ways passive people control others, this woman did not immediately concur with my findings! And indeed, passive people control others differently from those who blindly trust or those who aggressively distrust. Their "getting away" controls the access of others. Their "giving in" attempts to end any conflict as quickly as possible.

Blind trust often inspires people to move *toward* the conflicts of others in order to fix their problems and rescue them, but to move *away* from their own conflicts because they feel threatened. Passive distrust, however, prompts people to move away from all conflict and even the potential of conflict. Let's look at a few examples:

Getting away physically. People who passively distrust limit others' access to them by avoiding contact. As pointed out earlier, they may leave the room as soon as possible or simply choose not to attend an event.

A vivid memory from my childhood illustrates how I once physically distanced myself from a threatening situation. When I was about eleven years old, I played on a Little League baseball team called the Braves. We had one of the best pitchers in the league, some of the best hitters, and in the final week of the season, the best record. Our next game was with the Cubs, the second-place team. Do or die. Winner take all. (OK, so it wasn't the most important event in the Western hemisphere that decade, but you couldn't tell *us* that!)

In the fourth inning, the score was tied: one to one. The Cubs had a flame-throwing twelve-year-old named Billy Garrison on the mound. I was the second batter up. After the warm-up pitches, the first batter, Ken Dixon, stepped to the plate. We needed a run. Ken needed to get on base. A ball. A strike. Then, Ken got ready and Billy fired his fastball. I heard a "Thunk!" and saw Ken drop to the ground. The ball hit Ken squarely on the forehead. He was out cold.

The catcher and the umpire were kneeling over him in an instant. I was waiting in the on-deck circle, so I got there quickly, too. Then came the coach. The bump on Ken's forehead was already swelling. After a minute, he began to rouse. He sat in the dirt for another minute, then he started running—down the third-base line! Finally, Ken's direction was corrected and he arrived at first base amid the crowds' combined laughter and relief.

"Next batter!" the ump yelled.

Huh? Who, me? Wait a minute. Do you guys realize that my good friend, Ken Dixon, was just about decapitated by that fastball? No, I didn't say any of that, but I sure thought it! I didn't have time to consider all my options, but the Peace Corps was looking pretty good about then.

I *slowly* walked to the plate, my one and only goal being to avoid a tragic and messy death. Since I couldn't escape altogether, I positioned myself as far away from the plate as I possibly could. I found the very back, outside corner of the batter's box and stood on the lines. Then I leaned back as far as I could, held my arms as close to me as possible, and stood absolutely motionless. I was a veritable fortress!

Billy wound up for his first pitch. A fastball over. "Strike one." I didn't even breathe.

He threw again. "Strike two!" And again, "Strike three. You're out!" The umpire called.

No sweeter words were ever uttered. I had escaped impending death. Was my behavior passive? Petrified would be more accurate!

Getting away emotionally. If passive individuals must be in the same room with someone they consider threatening (which may include everyone who breathes!), they will avoid interaction. They may watch television, play with the dog, or read the paper. They may make conversation with children who seem safer than other adults. If asked a question or forced to enter a conversation, they will avoid eye contact and speak either quietly or quickly to "get it over with" and return to the relative safety of blending into the environment.

Giving in by being indecisive. When a passive person feels pressured for a decision—even a small one—and can't run or hide, they will stall. In times like these, a friend of mine says, "Wait! Wait! I'll figure it out! Just give me time." Some people laugh at him, and my friend laughs, too, to show that "it's no big deal." But the look in his eyes communicates fear, not humor. Assertiveness can bring ridicule, contradiction, or laughter from those deemed unsafe.

Perhaps passive people hope that stalling will give them time to figure out what to do. Perhaps they hope that someone else will get tired of waiting and go ahead and make the decision for them. Because they avoid stating their opinions, they don't know what they like or dislike. One man was asked: "Which do you like more: pizza or hamburgers?" He hesitatingly replied, "I'm not sure." Sadly, he responds this same way to any question about his preferences. His identity is so crushed that he really doesn't know.

Giving in by taking the blame. Another way to avoid conflict is to take all the blame. By instantly admitting, "It's all my fault," we assume the lesser pain (being blamed) instead of fac-ing the far greater threat of having to resolve the difficulty. We may have to talk through the problem with an untrustworthy person, speak the truth boldly, and take the risk of being hurt. Even though internalizing guilt seems to solve the short-term problem, it reinforces and prolongs the passive person's sense of shame and powerlessness.

PASSIVE-AGGRESSIVE: STRANGE BEDFELLOWS

Most observers of human behavior contend that truly passive people do not exist. Though continually repressed, the anger and hurt find expression, just not overtly. We often express anger in passive-aggressive behavior, a sort of indirect sabotage designed to hurt others without being caught. While the goal in such behavior is to punish, control, and take revenge, the passive person is afraid to do so openly.

These individuals often discover what makes their offenders angry and then surreptitiously "push their buttons." For instance, if a woman knows her husband can't stand to be late, she may take extra time with her hair, makeup, and clothes. As he fumes and glares at his watch every fifteen seconds, she says, "I'm so sorry I'm making us late. But you want me to look nice, don't you?"

Gossip provides another favorite ploy. Talking *about* someone instead of *to* them feels much safer than directly confronting the offender and the offense. Telling about someone else's disgusting behavior accomplishes the dual goals of winning sympathy and defaming the offender.

Sarcasm is one of the most common devices of passive-aggressive people. Sarcasm is directed toward an object and is designed to punish. Many consider sarcasm to be the perfect crime simply because it's so devastating, yet looks so innocent.

At church or at a party, a wife might say about her husband, "If Jim loses any more hair we won't need to buy a new heater. We can use his head as a solar reflection panel." Or a husband might say for all to hear at Thanksgiving dinner, "Honey, if you eat any more sweet potatoes we'll have to get one of those 'wide load' signs before we drive home."

In both instances, everyone would laugh at the "joke." And if the jokers were confronted with honest statements such as "You hurt my feelings," or if they noticed the target seemed hurt, they might say condescendingly, "Oh, you know I was just kidding. Can't you take a joke?" The wound had been inflicted. Innocence was affirmed. Passive aggression strikes again.

MAKING LIFE WORK

Those who passively distrust often try to control their own behavior through personal rituals, rigid rules, and severe punishments for even minor transgressions. Their narrow, isolated world allows for little objective input. They are self-contained. Without the freedom of expression which flows from feeling unconditionally loved, they are left to figure out how to make life work.

The rituals may be simple or elaborate. Passive distrust people may go through the same motions day after day: getting dressed in the same way, brushing their teeth in the same way, eating the same things at lunch, going to the same places. Such rituals are attempts to make sense out of life's uncertainties.

Passive people often surround these rituals with rigid rules to govern what is acceptable and unacceptable. These rules are usually coupled with punishments, and occasionally with rewards. The rules can relate to every aspect of life: like what, when, and how to eat, dress, and speak. When these rules are broken, the silent prisoners may vehemently condemn themselves, call themselves nasty names, and withhold pleasures and privileges as punishment. They vent all of the internalized anger on themselves, perhaps even inflicting physical harm because their self-hatred is so intense.

The rituals, rules, and punishment deepen this person's fear, shame, and bitterness. Life seems even more unfair, and others even more of a threat. The reasons to get away or give in continue to multiply.

Relating to God. Passive people usually assume that God is like the other threatening people in their lives. Assuming that God doesn't care and will only hurt them, they conclude it's best to avoid him. This perception, of course, may be subconscious. The person may not acknowledge these beliefs even if confronted with them. In fact, many Christians who are prone to passive distrust clearly articulate the grace, love, forgiveness, and kindness of God. After all, they're expected to say those things. To challenge them would create both internal and external conflicts—dangers to be avoided at all costs!

Passive people usually carry on an arm's-length relationship with God, much like they do with other authority figures. This kind of connection doesn't challenge the status quo and doesn't create conflict, but it also doesn't bring intimacy, freedom, and spontaneity. "Sure, I have a good relationship with the Lord," one woman related. "I try not to disappoint him. And I try to do what he expects of me." Her voice sounded sad and distant, an audible reflection of her relationship with God.

Many passive people incorporate the commands of Scripture right into their rigid rituals and rules. They can then feel justified and even self-righteous when they meet these standards. But when they fail, they feel even more shame and self-hatred. Now they not only punish themselves but they also feel sure that God is punishing them, too.

❖ ❖ ❖

Take Time to Reflect

Indicate whether or not the following statements are true of the way you usually respond:

yes   no   If I'm hurt in a relationship, I don't easily forget.

yes   no   When I'm upset with someone, my tendency is to withdraw.

yes   no   I often feel that others don't fully understand me.

yes   no   I have to admit that I do a poor job of handling conflict.

yes   no   I worry a lot about what will happen if I don't successfully change things.

yes   no   I often become angry at others, but just keep my feelings to myself.

yes   no   One of the ways I show my dissatisfaction with others is by giving them the silent treatment.

yes   no   My feelings can linger for days on end, well beyond the event that happened.

yes   no   I find myself rehashing what went wrong and how I can make things better.

yes   no   I withhold my emotions, especially my affection, whenever I'm upset.

yes   no   I'm pretty skilled in putting off conversations that I feel will result in an argument.

yes   no   I find it difficult to be decisive in simple decision-making matters.

yes   no   I may act nicely on the outside when I feel mad on the inside.

yes   no   I secretly enjoy seeing someone experience failure if I feel they deserve it.

yes   no   I get upset easily when I believe things are unfair.

yes   no   I may take the blame for something even though I know deep down it was someone else's fault.

yes   no   I often mask my feelings through sarcastic or humorous remarks.

yes   no   If I think others might like to know something negative about someone, I usually go ahead and tell them.

yes   no   People tell me I'm a pretty compulsive person; I like to do things a certain way.

yes   no   There are times when I feel I deserve to have bad things happen to me.

If you circle "yes" to ten or more of the above items, you have tendencies toward passive mistrust. Answering the following questions will shed more light on how trust operates in your day-to-day life (or in the life of someone close to you).

1. What is your payoff for being passive? What do you hope to get or avoid?

2. Do you feel manipulative? Why or why not?

3. How do you think of yourself? What is your sense of identity? What do you fear?

4. How do you try to control people or your environment?

5. What strengths does passivity bring to your relationship with God? What weaknesses do you experience?

6. How do you feel and act around passive people?

8

Charm and Venom

O UR COMMON CRAVING for safety seems to express itself in endless variations. We've explored those who are driven to please others in order to win approval, and those who feel compelled to avoid threats by getting away and giving in. Now we come to a third way.

Those who tend toward aggressive distrust have been hurt, too, but their subconscious response carries more vigor: "Never again! People only hurt me, but I won't let them do that anymore. I'll dominate, intimidate, and in some way, be superior." Should this mentality surface, it is quickly justified as being good and right and logical.

We usually think of aggression as a physical attack, and indeed, those who aggressively distrust may use this means of intimidation. They may victimize others by beating, gripping an arm, pinching, tickling, or sexually assaulting. Most aggressive individuals, however, more often use emotional intimidation. Criticism, fault-finding, public denunciation, sarcasm, scowls, a raised tone of voice, a look of contempt or disgust, are only a few of the many verbal and nonverbal messages designed to dominate others.

Like those who trust blindly, those who aggressively distrust move toward others, but not from a subservient stance. They feel a strong drive to dominate—although such behavior is not always overt. Their true colors come through under stress or in crisis. When aggressive people feel threatened, they must win.

Those who tend toward aggressive distrust do not come across as all gloom and doom. In fact, their sharp, quick minds enable them to be witty, charming, socially adept, and even affirming—when it serves their purposes. If they used only venom without charm, others would pull away far more readily. Instead, aggressive people send out a double message: "I love you. You're a jerk!" This affirmation draws people close (but not too close!) and the condemnation compels them to do whatever the aggressive person wants.

A few aggressive people exhibit extreme behavioral and character disorders. Some may be so self-focused as to become narcissistic. Others use people without regard for their feelings, even becoming sociopathic. How can these people hurt others so much? They simply don't care how others feel. They don't care about the painful consequences of their aggressive behavior in the lives of others.

We could easily view those who employ blind trust and passive distrust as victims and aggressive individuals as victimizers. Those labels seem to fit neatly. We must remember, however, that the first two groups generally smother or neglect others around them, while hidden underneath the iron-clad shell of every aggressive person lies someone who is wounded. He or she wants to be loved, but the fear of being hurt again drives others away.

"I'M RIGHT, YOU'RE WRONG!"

In aggressive distrust, power equals safety. They must be in control; they must be on top. Dan Allender describes this kind of person in his insightful book, *The Wounded Heart*. Allender observes that some sexual abuse victims adopt a "tough girl" role to protect themselves from further pain. He writes:

Internally, the Tough Girl is above her own feelings, suspicious of others' motives, and arrogant and angry in her evaluations of others. She views human need as childish and unnecessary.

She perceives others' movement toward her as their attempt to dominate; therefore, she spurns kindness and human warmth as not only unnecessary, but dangerous. She views compliments as a "buttering up before the kill," or a prelude to being used.

Arrogance shows itself beyond know-it-all-ism and a lack of interest in the thoughts and experiences of others. It is also manifested in a desire to control, or have a preeminent say in the activities of other people.[1]

This role is not the exclusive province of sexual abuse victims. Many others who have been emotionally and physically abused or neglected use intimidation to control people as well as keep them from getting too close.

Those who exercise blind trust and passive distrust internalize blame. They believe, "It's all my fault." This suits those who aggressively distrust just fine. In fact, they reinforce another person's internalized sense of guilt as they externalize blame: "It's all your fault!" With this perspective, aggressive people are usually cynical, suspicious, and critical of others.

One woman told our fellowship group that her husband's favorite word is "you," as in, "*You* messed up!" "Why can't *you* do anything right?" Whenever they have even the slightest disagreement, he points his finger literally and figuratively and says, "What's wrong with *you*? You're never satisfied!" In any conflict, of course, both sides almost invariably share culpability. This man seems unwilling to admit even the slightest contribution to the problem. His wife has become a "blame sponge," soaking up his criticism and condemnation.

Those who aggressively distrust base their identity in being right. Since they can't afford to be wrong, they will argue a point to the extremity of logic—and beyond—until they convince you they're right, or until they wear you down and you give in. Either way, they win.

Aggressive people are constantly checking themselves out on the pecking order to be sure they are "one up." If they feel powerful and appreciated, they can relax and be gracious. If threatened, they feel compelled to prove their own worth and put down others. One way to be one up is to be sure others are one down. Life becomes an adult game of leap frog, whether played at work, home, church, clubs, or in the neighborhood.

Marge, who works as a middle manager in a large company, fears being bypassed when promotions are granted. A mover and shaker, she has been promoted quickly at every step in her career. Immediately after each step up the career ladder, Marge assumes a warm, kind, and generous persona. She feels confident and powerful.

But after a while, the blush begins to wear off. Sensing the competition for the next level in the organizational chart, Marge becomes increasingly intense. She pours herself into her work and demands more of those under her. Their performance is a reflection on her, after all, and they'd better contribute! Whenever fellow managers are mentioned positively in conversations, she may agree they're doing well, but then subtly mentions their failures, character faults, or difficulties with subordinates. Marge is too slick to be obvious, but too driven to remain mute.

The career ladder offers one happy hunting ground for aggressive people. Information, academic degrees, possessions, and other status symbols may also be used as rungs on the way up for those prone to aggressive distrust. If they know more than others, if they have higher credentials, if they have something, anything over someone else, then they feel safer.

In a group discussion about this type of distrust, one man asked, "Do these people feel powerless? Is all this power, control, and intimidation a cover-up, or is it compensation for feelings of powerlessness?"

"Good question," I answered. We talked about the underlying motivation for a while. Some aggressive individuals seem to be aware of their underlying fear and their feeling of being out of control. Intimidating behavior would then be purposely chosen to compensate for these feelings.

Most of those who aggressively distrust, however, do not seem to be aware of their repressed fear, hurt, and anger. Their domination of others makes just as much sense to them as pleasing others does in blind trust, or getting away and giving in does in passive distrust. In their closed system, dominating others becomes the logical way of avoiding hurt and gaining power. While blind trust and passive distrust carry a plague of self-doubt, many who relate out of aggressive distrust could use a little more of it!

How do others respond to such aggressive intimidation? Usually by complying with the demands. Their aggressive counterparts perceive this compliance and mistakenly believe they have established good relationships with others. Most of these relationships, however, are not based on mutual respect, honesty, expressions of emotions and desires, and the resolution of conflict. To aggressive people, relationships are "dysfunctional dances," one demanding, others complying, each keeping step with the other.

Having developed few boundaries, those who blindly trust lack autonomy and the ability to make decisions. They check out what others want and simply comply. Passive people also lack boundaries, but they try to hide instead of actively pleasing others. Aggressive individuals construct rigid boundaries. They won't allow anyone to make decisions for them. They resent others' input (although they may verbalize appreciation). And they feel justified and comfortable in trampling on the boundaries of everyone else and making decisions for them.

Daily interactions reinforce these identity problems for those who aggressively distrust. As others comply with their dominance and express appreciation for their strong leadership, as their quick and accurate analysis meets an urgent need, and as they so effectively "get the job done right," aggressive people feel powerful and safe. Their ultimate goals have been accomplished.

THE INTIMIDATION FACTOR

Aggressive distrust produces some behaviors similar to blind trust, although their motives differ. Aggressive people also gravitate toward conflict between others, but with an aim to dominate the situation, resolve the problem, and prove their superiority. Because they feel threatened with admitting wrong, losing face, and losing power, they also avoid personal conflict. But the confrontational stance of aggressive distrust marks them as different: these individuals often create conflict as a means to intimidate others and keep them off balance.

Dominance and intimidation can be achieved through the following roles.

Field Marshal. Like Napoleon at Austerlitz or Patton at the Rhine, some who aggressively distrust assume command of everyone around them. They award quick and complete obedience with commendations. But sluggishness, variant opinions, and even questions may be interpreted as disloyalty—the worst possible trait, punishable by an immediate tongue-lashing or worse.

Because they tend to be bright, quick, sure of their solution to any problem, and able to give clear directions, Field Marshals often become leaders in whatever they do. These talented individuals receive praise, promotions, and awards for their ability to get the job done.

One woman smothered her children with direction and advice. No area of their lives was off-limits from her keen observation. When the children went off to college, she entered the business world. Without any formal training, this female Field Marshal quickly proved her superior leadership skills and determination to succeed. Frequent promotions allowed her to maximize her drives in this new arena of influence. Many people respected her. Many people feared her. Few could ignore her.

007. Some individuals prone to aggressive distrust seem more adept at covert operations. They avoid the center of attention, but still feel the need to dominate. They may withhold information, exaggerate the facts, and talk *about* people rather than *to* people. They master the art of passive-aggression.

"I can never get a straight answer from Mike," a business executive lamented. "In meetings, he always seems to have something to hide. Often I find out later about things Mike has known about—and knew I needed!—but didn't tell me. I think it makes him feel powerful."

He finally confronted Mike, but his co-worker again proved evasive. "Don't worry about anything. I'll be glad to tell you anything—anything at all!" But somehow, the executive knew he wasn't going to get anything more from Mike. Having confronted him, he'd probably get less.

A friend of mine entered a business arrangement with someone who seemed honest and upright, but turned out to be a 007. As the venture progressed, my friend had problems getting accurate accounting figures. "Oh, we're in good shape," 007 assured him every time questions were asked. "No problem." Finally, my friend's suspicions superseded these assurances. After calling in a lawyer and an outside accountant, he discovered that 007 had been milking the partnership for all he could get.

Professor. Information provides power for the Professor. Knowing everything they can possibly learn about every person and situation helps them feel more secure, less likely to be caught off guard. People who willingly give them information are befriended and appreciated. If someone withholds important information (all of which qualifies!), that person falls from grace and moves to the black list of suspected enemies. Professors eagerly gather information, but then jealously guard it and only grudgingly give it out. Knowledge means too much to be given away, except maybe in exchange for more.

Prophet. In a role closely associated with that of Professor, the Prophet uses knowledge and insight to make pronouncements about people. Displaying a knack for seeing through people and situations, these individuals seem clairvoyant. The problem is: they're often right! Prophets can size up a new person in the neighborhood in an instant; they can tell how a new teacher, boss, or pastor will behave before situations occur; they can predict which jobs or relationships will be best for acquaintances. The fact that Prophets prove to be right so often lends them an aura of power, and leads many others to believe whatever they say.

"You won't like the new minister," Betty told her friend.

Shocked by this pronouncement, the friend laughed, "You've only heard him one time, Betty! How can you say such a thing? I thought he was pretty good."

"Yeah, he was pretty good, but I can tell that he will cause division in the church," this Prophet replied with solemn sureness.

A few months later, the elders were divided over whether to take the church in a new direction for worship. At a congregational meeting, board members almost came to blows. Betty looked at her friend a few rows away with an expression that said, "I told you so."

"But how did you know?" she asked Betty after the meeting. Betty just laughed.

Judge, Jury, and Executioner. Here we come to probably the most common role played by people who aggressively distrust: to observe someone's behavior, pronounce it as deficient, and carry out the sentence of condemnation. This complex of behaviors vents and directs the stored-up anger of those who have aggressive distrust. They externalize blame.

They unleash criticism to create hurt and fear so that the recipient is more easily controlled.

Judges use sweeping, categorical, "always" and "never" statements to inflict wounds: "You never do anything right!" "You always whine about that!"

They use guilt-inducing words like "ought" and "should," often phrased in "you" messages which accuse and blame, rather than "I" messages which accept personal responsibility: "You ought to be ashamed of yourself!" "You shouldn't cry like that! Grow up!"

They interrupt and hurry people, showing disrespect for them and their feelings: "Hold it right there! Let me tell you the way it really is!" "I've got other stuff to do! Hurry up!" They raise their voices to intimidate and use facial expressions (like scowls and frowns) and body language (like hands on hips or arms folded) to communicate: "You are beneath me." "I don't respect you." "You've messed up!"

A friend of mine who is an accountant told me about his boss who seemed to pass judgment on their every move. The employees saw him behave very graciously to those outside the company, but he reserved his "fiery darts" for them. This man used almost every intimidating communication device, including public condemnation. New hires joined the company in hope, stayed in fear, and left with a mixture of relief (to be getting away) and guilt (because this employer convinced many of them that leaving would be a sin).

Unlike passive people who occasionally become aggressive when pushed "over the limit," those who play the role of Judge, Jury, and Executioner use criticism and condemnation as a lifestyle. They are not aberrations; they are the norm.

A BUSINESS RELATIONSHIP WITH GOD

As you might expect, those who aggressively distrust have problems relating to God. After all, only one person can take charge of the universe. And how can someone be submissive when his or her entire life is dedicated to dominating everyone and everything? These people are smart enough to realize early in their spiritual lives that "good Christians" need to look humble, and they want to be the "best Christians." Tension between the desire to dominate and the desire to look humble creates internal conflicts of large proportions.

This inner struggle can be resolved by avoiding the threat of intimacy and focusing on analysis and action. Instead of experiencing the love, grace, and gentleness of God, aggressive people analyze it. They may study every major doctrinal issue so they can understand it thoroughly—and dominate any discussion. While analysis is not as rich and fulfilling as genuine experience, it's certainly not as threatening. These individuals settle for a business relationship with God: "You do your part, God, and I'll do mine. You can count on me, and I sure hope I can count on you."

Aggressively distrustful people excel at action. They perceive the need, marshal the resources, command the troops, and get the job done right! The task may be evangelizing a neighborhood, raising money for the building fund, hosting a missions conference, or doing the accounting. They love to be busy. They feel comfortable with analysis but reflection calls for being open and honest about motives, hurts, and desires. It's to be avoided at all costs.

Those prone to aggressive distrust may think they have a close relationship with God. They expect him to perform for them—like everybody else does. When the sovereign God lets them down, they may become furious. On the other hand, aggressive people may reframe the situation to show that God did what they wanted after all. Again, they have to win, no matter who's playing the game.

Leadership and church management tend to be a favorite sphere of activity for these individuals. It allows them to use their finely tuned skills, drive, and ability to control others. Their effectiveness in church activities, like business or other venues, leads to appreciation and more opportunities to exercise power.

While aggressive people gravitate toward positions of leadership in the church, their service may be another way to maintain control. Some exercise this power from behind the scenes but are glad when others find out how they've effected change. Others more overtly seek the limelight of honor, praise, and appreciation.

Author, speaker, and social commentator Charles Colson tasted the deception of power as part of Nixon's White House staff. In *Power Religion*, Colson notes how this quest for authority over others convolutes genuine spiritual leadership: "The lure of power can separate the most resolute of Christians from the true nature of Christian leadership, which is service to others. It's difficult to stand on a pedestal and wash the feet of those below."[2]

In group meetings those who aggressively distrust have to give all the answers—except for 007, who sits quietly analyzing everyone's responses. Being one up and being in command has ceased being optional; aggressive people must dominate in every arena. God is not willing to play this power game forever. Ultimately, he will graciously allow even the hardest working, most competent individuals to come to their end so that they will trust him.

God wants to create both inner strength and dependence in all of us. He will orchestrate events in his timing, in his way, and according to his purposes to teach us our need for his grace and power. In rare flashes of insight, people who aggressively distrust may feel broken and contrite before God. They may feel sorrow for intimidating others and using God to accomplish their purposes.

This window of understanding may not stay open long, however. Such tender feelings make aggressive people feel weak and vulnerable. It's much easier to dominate. But God can get through over and over again if we will only listen and believe in his goodness, safety, and strength.

❖ ❖ ❖

Take Time to Reflect

Indicate whether or not the following statements are true of the way you usually respond:

yes no If I think something needs to be said, I come right out with it.

yes no I like to take the lead in relationships.

yes no I become irritated with people who can't face the facts.

yes no I'm not easily intimidated by others.

yes no I tend to be mistrustful of people who are always nice; it seems as if they're trying to manipulate others.

yes no I let people know exactly where I stand on an issue.

yes no Being in control of situations stimulates me.

yes no When there is a job to be done, I like to jump right in and do it.

yes no You could describe me as a competitive sort of person.

yes no I'm good at out-dueling others in debates.

yes no I prefer to view a situation with logic, not with emotion.

yes no I can be quite convincing when I get into an argument.

yes no I can't stand to have people point out my faults.

yes no I believe that the more knowledge you have about a situation, the better off you are.

yes no It doesn't take me long to form an opinion.

yes   no   Even when I'm trying to be considerate of others, I'm accused of being too aggressive in my reactions.

yes   no   I often explode when I'm angry.

yes   no   I get impatient with those who have trouble making decisions.

yes   no   I have a hard time relaxing; I like to be doing something.

yes   no   I tend to see things as either right or wrong, black or white.

If you circle "yes" to ten or more of the above items, you show tendencies toward aggressive mistrust. Answering the following questions will shed more light on how trust operates in your day-to-day life (or in the life of someone close to you).

1. What payoff do you expect for being aggressive? What do you hope to gain or avoid?

2. Do you use any of these roles to control people?
   • Field Marshal
   • 007
   • Judge, Jury, and Executioner
   • Professor
   • Prophet

3. Do you understand why you act the way you do? Explain.

4. What is your sense of identity? How would you describe yourself?

5. What possible strengths does aggressive distrust bring to your relationship with God? What are some possible weaknesses?

6. How do you feel and act around aggressive people?

9

"Turbo Trust"

*A*FTER I HAD EXPLAINED blind trust, passive distrust, and aggressive distrust to our fellowship group, we discussed the typical fears and compulsions of each. We talked about the various defenses used to avoid more hurt or the different methods to exert control. After a lengthy discussion, I noticed that Mary looked a little desperate and anxious. She blurted out, "Isn't there any good kind of trust? Am I doomed to be one of these three forever?"

Apologies seemed to be in order. I had failed to include perceptive trust in our overview. And without a sense of hope, we all begin to feel desperate and anxious!

A friend of mine tried to remember the four kinds of trust. Matt came pretty close until the last one. "Let's see, there's blind trust, people who don't trust, mean trust, and uh... oh, yeah, TURBO TRUST!" Turbo trust... not bad. I kind of like it! But perceptive trust is a bit more descriptive, even if it sounds relatively dull.

Because we often view life in black or white, we may assume that the first three kinds of trust are all bad, while perceptive trust is all good. Let me state clearly what perceptive trust is not. It's not total safety, absolutely accurate perception, perfect peace, or complete freedom from hurt and anger. This fourth type of trust is not the diametric opposite of all our false beliefs and fears. It's not some state you achieve—like some paradise on earth—once you've dealt with every one of your personal issues.

Then what is it? Simply put, perceptive trust is the ability to discern others' trustworthiness—or lack thereof—and the courage to take appropriate risks. One possible synonym would be "wisdom." People who trust perceptively avoid polarized thinking and recognize the ambiguities and inconsistencies of people, situations, and life. They remember that every person, even a trustworthy one, sometimes disappoints us.

A CREATURELY PERSPECTIVE

As members of the human race, we are all imperfect, frail, and wayward. The prophet Jeremiah recognized human nature when he recorded: "The heart is more deceitful than all else and is desperately sick; who can understand it?" (Jer 17:9). Only God is completely trustworthy, even though we often fail to understand his purposes or his ways.

Many verses in Scripture describe the Lord as unfathomable, undefinable, and ineffable. The apostle Paul wrote, "Oh, the depth of the riches both of the wisdom and knowledge of God! How unsearchable are his judgments and unfathomable his ways" (Rom 11:33). And in the Old Testament, Isaiah penned God's words: "'For my thoughts are not your thoughts, neither are your ways my ways,' declares the Lord. 'For as the heavens are higher than the earth, so are my ways higher than your ways, and my thoughts than your thoughts'" (Is 55:8-9).

Only a few years ago, I struggled with my own sense of identity. As a genuine, bona fide, blue-chip blind-trust person, I felt compulsively driven to please every member of the human race, accomplish goals, gain status, and in general be the hero of the world! In my spare time, I blamed myself for the problems of other people. For fun, I felt guilty for everything I said or did. Sounds like a great time, huh?

After a few weeks of studying Paul's letter to the Ephesians, I made a remarkable discovery: that God loves me, has forgiven me, and has accepted me by his grace. New truths? Not exactly. New to me? Well, yes, kind of, new because I was starting to grasp it. Actually, I had been telling people these principles for a long time, but I hadn't really believed them. Perhaps a timely Bible study can open a new door in your own life.

Anyway, I began to wonder how I could remember these truths whenever I felt so driven or guilty or afraid. (Like all the time!) So I wrote and memorized a simple statement:

I am completely and absolutely loved, forgiven, and accepted by God's grace.

Those dozen words meant the world to me! A couple of years later, I met Robert S. McGee at a conference. The founder and president of Rapha, a health care organization, Robert filled in a lot of the blanks for me with his book, *The Search for Significance.* These simple truths form the foundation of a sound, biblical identity: We are loved, forgiven, and accepted by God through Jesus Christ.

As we become increasingly convinced of our security in Christ, we can be more objective about our sinfulness, strengths, and weaknesses. These realities are put in perspective. We no longer have to be the best; we no longer see ourselves as incorrigibly hopeless. In the same vein, Paul encouraged the believers in Rome to see themselves accurately: "For through the grace given to me I say to every man among you not to think more highly of himself than he ought to think; but to think so as to have sound judgment, as God has allotted to each a measure of faith" (Rom 12:3).

Having sound judgment means realistically appraising who we are. That appraisal—which is undergirded and fostered by our security in Christ—then leads to more perception and peace. Rather than being trapped in a vicious cycle, we find ourselves riding on a charitable cycle.

The more secure we are in the grace of God, the less we feel compelled to live by rituals and rules. We learn to listen to the Spirit's leading, as well as to the sound advice of other believers. The Lord is infinitely creative. He leads us into all kinds of relationships and situations where we can learn to know him more intimately and serve him more effectively.

These opportunities, however, don't always assume the shape and form of the obviously positive. In his sovereign wisdom, God sometimes leads us into painful and difficult circumstances to accomplish his primary goals: his glory and our growth. The Christian life really proves to be an "exciting adventure" as we listen to our Lord and follow him, one step at a time.

As we travel down this road with one another, our growing security in Christ allows us to be more honest about our feelings as well as our own responsibility for past actions. Many of us endured painful childhood experiences which resulted in repressed emotions. Children usually aren't able to select which ones to repress and which ones to feel, so we tend to repress them all to some degree. Grieving allows us to appropriately acknowledge and process the hurts of the past so they do not compound the hurts—and the joys—of the present.

Perceptive trust also allows us to take responsibility for our behavior and to set limits on our readiness to accept blame (we'll talk more about how to do this in the remaining chapters). We learn that the feelings and behaviors of others are not our responsibility. The believer is gradually empowered by an inner strength to make and carry out decisions.

Desperation often fuels our earliest attempts, while anger at the past and hope for the future keep us paddling down midstream. During the latter phases of our journey, we feel steadily strengthened by a calm assurance of God's goodness and sovereignty.

Throughout the journey, God is always at work in the believer to accomplish his purposes. His Spirit provides the necessary wisdom and strength for each step, along with the courage to keep going when we grow discouraged. We can learn to experience our identity in Christ even at the beginning of our process of learning how to trust wisely.

VALUING RELATIONSHIP OVER RULES

The goal in perceptive trust is to *love* others, not *control* them. Notice: the goal is not to *trust* them. Trusting untrustworthy people is not virtuous; it's downright foolish. But we can love and forgive even those who break our trust, perhaps allowing them to experience some of the consequences of their behavior for their own sake.

People who blindly trust confuse rescuing with love. They believe they serve others best by bailing them out, enabling them, preventing them from being responsible, and experiencing the consequences of their behavior. The unspoken hope, of course, is that the rescued will appreciate the rescuer. As those who trust blindly gain perception and wisdom, they will feel less compelled to rescue others for their own sakes. They will learn to speak the truth instead of always pleasing others. They will be able to let others suffer the consequences of their own behavior. Could that be loving? Yes. Christ always let people make their own choices and experience the consequences (Lk 18:18-30; Jn 6:66; 13:27; Mk 6:1-6).

People who passively distrust confuse pity with love. Passive by nature, they wait for others to act first. If others feel sorry for them and thus treat them gently, they will respond in kind. This gentle waltz may not hurt anybody, but it lacks genuine affection, honesty, integrity, and conflict resolution.

People who aggressively distrust mistake dominance and compliance for love. They move toward people to control them, not letting others make decisions for themselves. One intimidating husband gruffly told me, "Sure I love her, but she needs direction. She can't make a decision on her own. What would she do without me?" (Be a person, maybe?)

People whose trust is tempered with perception work at

communicating clearly and appropriately. They use "I feel," "I want," and "I will" statements to take responsibility for their feelings, desires, and behavior. They observe the responses of others to determine if and how they prove trustworthy. They are "wise as serpents and harmless as doves" (Mt 10:16, NKJV).

Perceptive people feel less driven to win at all costs or hide from all threats. They can wisely decide how to use their strengths more effectively. Because their security is not threatened by their rank or the pecking order, they can be good leaders as well as good followers.

Finally, people who wisely trust acknowledge the risks entailed by relationships, but realize that some of these risks are appropriate. When conflicts arise, they learn to address them with honesty and humility. When wrong, they repent; when wronged, they acknowledge the hurt and choose to forgive.

By allowing others to make their own choices instead of controlling them, we run significant risks. Some individuals will leave us, some will attack us, some will befriend us. Most won't know what to do! To stop controlling people requires tremendous inner strength. That fortitude grows as we exercise our growing perception, wisdom, and security in Christ.

People who are learning perceptive trust realize that a few particulars about God and humanity may be certain, but much remains unfathomable. Our trust hinges not on "figuring him out" but on God's sovereignty and goodness. Rituals and rules offer only a shadow of reality. Paul admonished the Christians in Colossae about meaningless rituals and empty rules:

Therefore let no one act as your judge in regard to food or drink or in respect to a festival or a new moon or a Sabbath day—things which are a mere shadow of what is to come; but the substance belongs to Christ.... If you have died with Christ to the elementary principles of the world, why, as if you were living in the world, do you submit yourself to decrees, such as, "Do not handle, do not taste, do not touch!" (which all refer to things destined to perish with the using)—in accordance with the commandments and teachings of men? These are matters which have, to be sure, the appearance of wisdom in self-made religion and self-abasement and severe treatment of the body, but are of no value against fleshly indulgence. **Colossians 2:16-17, 20-23**

Paul concludes his argument by explaining that Christ himself is the object of our trust and affection: "If then you have been raised up with Christ, keep seeking the things above, where Christ is, seated at the right hand of God. Set your mind on the things above, not on the things that are on earth. For you have died and your life is hidden with Christ in God. When Christ, who is our life, is revealed, then you also will be revealed with him in glory" (Col 3:1-4).

We can learn that God desires an intimate relationship with us. We can respect him as a powerful and loving father, even crying out as adopted sons and daughters, "Abba! Father!" which could be translated Daddy (see Rom 8:15).

As this relationship with our heavenly Father becomes more real to us, our prayers will incorporate listening as well as praise and petition. Convinced of God's strength and goodness, we can be honest with him. We can accept both good and bad. When we experience the pain of spiritual conflict (Eph 6:10-18) or pruning (Jn 15:1-8), we can learn to trust in our Father's essential kindness and loving purposes.

Perceptive trust also helps us to learn that every "spiritual impression" does not necessarily stem from God. Just as we need to let others prove their trustworthiness, we are encouraged by the apostle John to "test the spirits" (1 Jn 4:1) to see if they are from God. Learning how to trust with godly discernment helps us to experience more and more of the rich reality of God. He desires us as a proud Papa; we respond to him as little children.

We can learn and grow in our ability to trust perceptively. It is the road, as well as the destination of our progress. Don't expect to jump from blind trust, passive distrust, or aggressive distrust directly to perceptive trust. Rather than a doorway through which we walk, the journey requires skills which we acquire and develop—slowly and carefully. The last section of the book will focus on how to change.

Growth never comes easily. It takes hard work to reflect often, to read and learn new principles, and especially, to make the hard choices that lay down the stepping stones of progress. It's hard, but it's worth it. The benefits of clarity of thought, the freedom to make your own choices and live with the consequences, and the depth of relationships with God and others are well worth the trouble.

❖ ❖ ❖

Take Time to Reflect

1. How would perceptive trust help you to handle the complexities of life?

2. Do you think perceptive people are happy? Why or why not?

3. How would perceptive people think of themselves?

4. List some possible strengths in a perceptive person's relationship with God, as well as some possible weaknesses.

6. How can this type of person develop "the strength to be weak"?

7. How do you typically feel and act around people who trust perceptively?

PART THREE

❖ ❖ ❖

Growing in Trust

10

Prognosis for Change

AFTER HEARING MY TALK about perceptive trust, one woman impatiently asked, "All this sounds good to me! But how do you get there?"

We all find ourselves somewhere along this process of learning and growing. All of us have relationships with people who have trust problems. Some of these individuals may be only mildly manipulative, condemning, ingratiating, or secretive, but some of them go first class!

You may be a single woman with a boyfriend who trusts blindly. He wants too much from you; he needs you. At times you feel indispensable and strong because you help him; other times you feel trapped and suffocated by his constant demands and manipulative self-pity and anger. What's the payoff for you in this relationship? Is it the strength you get by being needed? What keeps you from changing? Is it that you would feel guilty if you set limits and turned down some of his requests?

You may work under an aggressive, dominant, intimidating employer. He's charming, witty, and generous one day, and a tiger the next. He questions your intelligence, attacks your competence and skills, and impugns your judgment. Your confidence ebbs and flows based on his moods. What's the payoff for you? You may be living for the compliments which send occasional rays of sunshine into your stormy relationship. What keeps you from being strong and independent? Are you afraid you couldn't function properly without his supervision?

You may have a passive spouse who avoids conflict, including any conversation with the slightest hint of disagreement. She won't even talk about problems. She just gives in and says, "I don't care. Do whatever you think best." When you pursue your wife to talk about some difficulty, she becomes emotionally paralyzed and stone quiet. Your anger only makes her withdraw more, so you feel confused. You can't talk to resolve any problems and you can't express your anger.

What's the payoff for you? You may sincerely want to resolve problems, but you may also enjoy a sense of superiority and control over the household. What keeps the relationship with your wife from growing and changing? Perhaps you've treated her like a child for so long that relating to her like an adult would threaten the stability of the relationship.

In countless scenarios, each one of us will stay the way we are until something forces us to change—perhaps a crisis, God, or both. We won't make hard choices until we have to. When our drive to change surpasses our comfort level, then we need to be as objective as possible about ourselves, our relationships, and our situation.

DESPERATION: THE COMMON DENOMINATOR OF CHANGE

Why do some people enter the growth process while others refuse? Why do some people make progress more quickly than others? Why do some people become much healthier while others remain stuck in hopelessness, bitterness, and fear?

People develop a determination to change for many different reasons. They may be fed up with a spouse. Perhaps they've been depressed for many years and can't stand to feel so helpless, hopeless, and lethargic anymore. Some people regret having alienated those who love them. Others realize they're treating their children the same way their parents treated them, even though they swore they never would.

Whatever the reason, we determine to change because we are desperate. We have to get help. We simply can't go on the way life has been. As I listen to men and women tell why they're getting counseling or joining a support group, the stories vary widely, but the look in their eyes tells a similar tale. They have denied the hurt and anger as long as they could. They have put up with someone's abusive behavior so long, they thought they would break. They despise themselves for their own shameful ways of treating people.

Denying, excusing, and minimizing have put off making payment, but the interest on the debt has been steadily compounding—daily, monthly, yearly.

Our determination to change can be quite fragile, however. The fears can rise again and overwhelm us, shutting down our hard-won progress. Specific fears may crop up, such as, "What if my husband found out I told you about this?" Or we may suffer amorphous feelings of dread, confusion, and doom. We fear "breaking the family secret," surfacing and being overwhelmed by long-repressed hurt and anger, being laughed at, and being misunderstood. We fear quick and simple answers. We fear being "fixed" by someone. And we fear what being "healthy" really means: "Will I have to relate to my husband (or wife, or child, or parent, or boss, etc.) differently? What if they hurt me again? What if I can't do it?"

All of these fears can keep us stuck. Addressing them proves to be a vital part of the process—like taking down the sandbags after the threat of flooding has passed. Our desperation keeps us moving, while other motivations of hope, anger, and love fuel our progress.

ROADBLOCKS TO CHANGE

A particular viewpoint often permeates our thought processes, but we aren't even aware of it. Yet this shadowy perspective may have a stranglehold on our growth process. It seems perfectly legitimate. It feels good. But this perspective prevents us from making the choices that lead to help and strength. It is the "victim mentality."

The wound of trust betrayed goes deep. Having been roughly handled or avoided by those who were supposed to provide care violates a person's trust. Victims feel hurt and angry because of serious offenses; they want things to be made right for them. This desire, however, is so powerful that it transcends expectations. Christian psychologist and author Dr. Larry Crabb calls it "demandingness."

Victims demand justice. Most wounded people possess a very strong sense of right and wrong. Righting wrongs, especially wrongs done to us, is not a calm, detached activity. It becomes a crusade! It must be done, and we won't rest until we've accomplished it.

A few months ago, my son had problems with another boy at school who picked on him. When I got home from work, Taylor was still fuming, "I'm going to knock his head off!"

I figured he probably needed to find a more acceptable solution. "Well, Son, that may not be the best course of action. Maybe we can come up with a better plan."

Taylor didn't like my suggestion. In righteous indignation, he said, "But, Dad, the Bible says, 'Vengeance is mine, I will repay,' and I'm going to repay him big time!"

At least my son was using the Scriptures as a part of his decision-making process. "Son, you need to look at that verse again." I found my Bible and turned to Romans 12. "Look at it right here. It says, "'Vengeance is mine, I will repay,' *says the Lord.*"

Taylor instantly realized that this slight clarification short-circuited his plan to murder his classmate. "Shoot!" he said disgustedly.

My son's lust for revenge closely parallels the desire of many of us. Adults usually learn ways of taking revenge which aren't so obviously vindictive. We gossip, we use sarcasm, we don't answer a question, we dilly-dally if we know that lateness bothers the other person. Such behaviors prove so effective because they accomplish the desired purpose of hurting someone while we look so innocent. But other actions show no subtlety at all. We may use open criticism, hateful looks, yelled epithets, and physical blows to take revenge for real or perceived wounds. The victim then becomes the perpetrator, whether subtly or overtly.

Victims demand compensation. For justice to be served, victims demand to be compensated for their losses. They may focus the demand on the one who caused the injury, but often the victim excuses that person and expects anyone and everyone else to compensate. This free-floating demand lends victims a hard edge of anger, resentment, and self-pity.

On the vague scales of subjective justice, victims expect others to give them whatever they want. After all, they deserve to be happy, to be left alone when they don't want to talk, to be listened to when they do. People ought to feel sorry for them, overlook their errors, and let them be irresponsible with no consequences.

Victims demand guarantees. Many wounded people insist on a risk-free life, which seems only right for all the hurt they've experienced. They've already hurt enough. Surely people should be willing to guarantee such reasonable requests as unconditional love, a hassle-free life, enough money to do what they want, a comfortable home, a job with good pay, adjustable hours and a kind boss, understanding friends, and anything else that feels good.

An inherently passive perspective and lifestyle produces demands for justice, compensation, and guarantees. Instead of "I'd better make good choices, forgive those who hurt me, and take responsibility for my life," those with a victim mentality point the verbal finger at others. They say, in effect, "They'd better make me happy, leave me alone, do what I want, get others to care for me," or more pointedly, "You'd better do all I want so I can be happy."

Demandingness blocks growth and change. It clouds our perception and keeps us from learning to trust wisely. As long as we focus on what others must do to make us happy, we will neglect taking responsibility for making the hard choices.

Our prognosis for change closely parallels how clearly we grasp the issue of our demands—whether it be for justice, compensation, or guarantees. Our level of demandingness can be slowly lowered as our level of safety increases. Also, as our demands recede, they are replaced by those traits which are most fulfilling and winsome: thankfulness, contentment, forgiveness, and genuine love.

VARYING DEGREES OF HOPE

Many factors influence our capacity to change and grow. Each type of mistrust, however, possesses its own unique assets and liabilities, specific needs to be addressed and strengths to be channeled in order to learn to trust perceptively. And each one has a somewhat different prognosis.

Blind trust. Though people who trust without question may begin the process as the least objective of the three types, they usually have the highest probability for growth. These individuals tend to be very active, even overly responsible, but this energy can be channeled into making the hard decisions which ultimately promote healing.

A friend of mine epitomized this energy. Ann was a compulsive fixer and rescuer. She felt responsible for everybody's problems in her family, church, neighborhood, and workplace. She was always quick to offer advice and a helping hand—even when no one asked for it! As my friend entered the recovery process, all these mental and physical energies were then directed toward healing. Ann read voraciously; she rarely missed a group meeting; and she was determined to make better choices.

Their desire to please can be a hindrance if the one who blindly trusts tries only to "say the right things" and "do the right things" to please a counselor or group leader. If someone addresses this compulsion to please, however, it can open up a window on the person's motivation. They could take advantage of this checkpoint to ask themselves, *Why am I saying or doing this? Do I just want that person's approval, or is it the right thing, whether he or she approves or not?*

One of the toughest barriers in blind trust involves the difficulty of separating from an enmeshed relationship. These individuals may continue an unhealthy relationship because they fear losing the sense of identity they gain from the other person. The other person may skillfully play on the overly trusting person's shame and desire to please. They may say, "You're so selfish!" "You don't care about me anymore!" "How could you do this to me?" "A good Christian wouldn't treat me this way!"

Such statements pour verbal salt—or hydrochloric acid!—into existing wounds. Those who blindly trust may have very little sense of identity, but they certainly don't want to be seen as selfish, mean, and heartless. To the ears of a pleaser, these are very manipulative words!

In order to continue the growth, pleasers need frequent megadoses of objectivity. They need to see how their compulsion to please and their enmeshment actually prove harmful to others as well as to themselves. This dawning realization proves essential to the tough decisions which these individuals need to make. Objectivity leads to many disappointments. Those who were once blindly trusted must now be seen as less than perfectly trustworthy. Rather than deferring to a supposedly trustworthy person to decide for them, pleasers begin to bear more responsibility in decision-making.

Passive distrust. Passive people view life with an inherent sense of hopelessness, but their objectivity gives them a fair prognosis for change. Passivity is their primary line of defense. Clear, specific, attainable goals can counterbalance this weakness. Passive people are easily overwhelmed, but if they can identify realistic expectations, they are much more likely to take productive steps.

People who passively distrust usually feel alone and abandoned. They have survived by "being out of people's way." While isolation has prevented some hurt, it has also prevented intimacy, confidence, and a strong sense of identity. Such people often respond to encouragement with genuine surprise.

After clearly outlining some steps he needed to take in his relationship with his father, a man in our support group said dejectedly, "I just don't think I can do it. Every time I try, I just shut down. I wilt. I can't say a word. I feel like a fool. I don't want to do that again."

Another member of the group affirmed him. "Peter, you've made a lot of progress so far." She remembered and described several hard decisions this man had made. "You can do this one, too. I know you can."

As his past times of strength were being recounted, Peter could hardly believe that anyone had paid attention to him. "You remembered all that?" he asked, on the verge of tears.

"Yes, and we'll all remember this one, too!" the woman remarked with both strength and kindness in her voice.

Peter felt affirmed and encouraged. He didn't follow through perfectly; he made some mistakes, but he moved ahead. Without any encouragement, he may not have taken that step.

Passive people have made a career of avoiding risks. Now they must learn to take calculated risks. They need to redirect their perception of hopelessness and channel it into determining specific action. The steps may be small, but they can be steps forward nonetheless.

All three types need accountability as a stimulus for follow-through, but passive people require more. Simple questions will help clarify goals: "What do you need to do now?" "How will you do it?" "When will you do it?" After the proposed action, follow-up questions as rudimentary as "How did it go?" let passive people know they will need to give a report.

Accountability is not the norm for most of us. It can seem like meddling. Indeed, holding people accountable does equate with meddling if they didn't request it. We may need to specifically ask others to hold us accountable, especially for particularly fearful events.

One woman in our group told us she was going to talk to her father about his emotional neglect. "I'm really scared to say anything to him about my hurt," she said honestly. "I'm afraid I'll back out, so would you ask me about it next week? That will help me go through with the conversation."

We all nodded. Several voiced assurances. At the beginning of the next meeting, someone asked her, "Tell us about your talk with your dad. How did it go?" She then related her painful conversation with him. Her dad hadn't responded the way she had hoped, but she'd learned a lot about herself and him by being honest for a change. "I don't know if I could have done it if I hadn't known you were all praying for me—and that you'd ask me about it tonight. That really helped. Thanks."

Aggressive distrust. Those who aggressively distrust face the greatest challenge in making progress because they have the most trouble admitting their needs. Aggressive people have carefully constructed a world of power, intimidation, and charm in order to dominate others. Admitting their needs would cause this house of cards to collapse.

Growth and change for those who aggressively distrust means grieving losses, forgiving, and taking responsibility. Progress also includes the possibility or the fear of losing the status attained by their drive, initiative, and finely honed skills.

Aggressive individuals often say they're receptive to new ideas, including ideas about emotional healing. Indeed, they may become students of these concepts—not for their own healing but to know more than someone else. Their goal once again is power and domination, not humility and healing.

Intervention is often necessary for those who aggressively distrust. God can intervene by bringing crises into their lives, but I have seen several of these types experience trauma after trauma without crying out for help. Other people may initiate the intervention, but their version of the truth is terribly threatening to the aggressive person, who often counter-attacks. One man told me about his employer: "She seems to take criticism really well, but you'd better watch out a couple of weeks later! She'll make you pay for ever doubting or questioning any decision she makes."

The prognosis for people who aggressively distrust is not hopeless, however. The protective shell can crack; a sense of desperation can take hold. When this happens, these individuals need the same ingredients of comfort, confrontation, courage, and clear goals, but they will come at these issues from a different direction. They will need to lower their production goals, take time to listen to people instead of ordering them around, and channel their drive into healing themselves and serving others.

BECOMING OBSERVANT

Our prognosis for change improves when we take time to recognize patterns in our responses to certain kinds of people, even predictable responses to particular individuals. If we are observant, we can also detect the ways others respond to us. Our self-pity may elicit from others rescuing behavior; our passivity may tell others we don't care about them; our angry tone and criticism may produce fear in others.

Perhaps you found your own patterns of behavior reflected in the preceding chapters. You may have understood more clearly why you feel and act the way you do. As I mentioned in chapter one, very few of us exhibit purely one kind of trust or distrust in every situation. In fact, we usually respond to specific individuals in different ways. For instance, we may use passive distrust with all authority figures, but relate with aggressive distrust with those under our supervision.

All-or-nothing thinking leads to extremes and wide pendulum swings. Sam is very passive, quiet, and withdrawn in most relationships, but when he feels he's getting close with a woman, he becomes domineering. Sam feels like he has to dominate her. If she doesn't become virtually his pawn or slave, he dumps her. (Of course, most women dump this guy when he switches gears so quickly.)

Jane is a fixer who thrives on being needed. When anybody needs help, she's quick to suggest solutions and even be the solution to their problems. Jane's assertiveness, however, completely evaporates around strong, dominant people. Her fear of these individuals paralyzes her, even if they've proven to be safe and trustworthy authority figures.

People often wonder about relationship patterns. They may ask, "Do aggressive people try to find passive people so they can dominate them?" I hear the converse question less often, "Are passive people attracted to aggressive people?" Natural attraction seems to occur in relationships just as it does in nature. In order to feel powerful, aggressive people need passive people who are easily intimidated. They may despise irresponsibility or neediness, but aggressive people gravitate toward those who are passive because they're easy marks. Their loathing for such weakness just provides more ammunition for intimidating others.

I find it more difficult to answer this question: "Are passive people drawn to aggressive people?" When I asked this in a recent seminar, most people nodded. One woman, however, angrily shook her head. Both responses can be right. Passive people may hate being controlled, but they usually fear taking responsibility even more. A sense of helplessness, hopelessness, worthlessness, and powerlessness combine to lock the passive person into relationships with powerful, aggressive people.

Although often manipulated and victimized, the passive person perceives this power as a form of safety. They escape having to make hard decisions, take the blame for mistakes, or even voice opinions.

WHAT'S YOUR PATTERN?

What are the complexities and natural attractions in your life? What is your dominant type of trust or mistrust? As you've read the various descriptions throughout this book, you've probably thought of many people in your life who exhibit blind trust, passive distrust, and aggressive distrust. You may have thought of a few people who seem pretty adept at perceptive trust. Take a few minutes to list people in your life who seem to fall into each category.

Blind trust (driven to please, fix, rescue, trusting untrustworthy people):

Passive distrust (avoid conflict at all costs, "lost children," fearful and withdrawn):

Aggressive distrust (intimidating, dominating, charm and venom):

Perceptive trust (wise, honest, strong, kind):

Now take some time to describe their actions toward you and your reactions and responses toward them. Your drive to succeed, your need to please, and your compulsion to hide will make more sense as you list and describe each relationship. I asked a friend to complete a worksheet on her patterns. Cindy's responses may provide a helpful example.

My dominant trust type __blind trust__.

Person	Trust type	They act toward me...	I act toward them...
Randy (first husband)	Aggressive Distrust (007)	Was very attentive and kind until we married, then passive aggressive, adultery	I believed him too long. I felt guilty when I first suspected something was wrong. Later I was hurt, angry, and bitter.
mother	Passive Distrust	distant, permissive, pitiful	I felt (and still feel) responsible to make her happy, but I have to read her mind to do it.
father	Aggressive Distrust (Field Marshall)	Sometimes warm and loving, sometimes harsh and demanding	I have always wanted his love so much, but I'm really afraid of him.
brother	Passive Distrust	pitiful, angry	I felt both angry with him, but also responsible for him.
Janice boss	Aggressive Distrust	cool, demanding	OK if she's nice or away on business, but afraid and compliant around her.
Philip son	Blind Trust	helpful, strong, fun, affectionate	We are very close, we understand each other very well. Can read each other's minds.
Pat daughter	Passive Distrust	compliant, distant, needy	I get impatient with her. I'm often demanding.

Person	Trust type	They act toward me...	I act toward them...
Shannon friend	Blind Trust	understanding, helpful	We are close. Vulnerable with each other.
God	Perceptive Trust	I'm not sure; my perception of God is a blend of my father and mother.	Sometimes very close; sometimes very distant. Confusing.

This simple exercise helped Cindy identify similar feelings she often had toward several people in her life. The patterns of her responses to each type of mistrusting person helped her also make better decisions about setting boundaries with some, being more assertive with others, moving toward some, and being more cautious with others.

Our past choices may have seemed good to us at the time. In fact, they often seemed like our only option. Objectively seeing the hurts, strained relationships, and lost opportunities of past decisions helps to steel our commitment to change. Experiencing the emotional and relational benefits of good decisions also motivates us. The positive memories coupled with the negative pain usually stir up a sense of anger at the past and hope for the future—a combination which generates the energy, courage, and strength we need to change.

❖ ❖ ❖

Take Time to Reflect

1. Fill out this worksheet to observe your patterns of trust and mistrust:

My dominant trust type _____.

Person	Trust type	They act toward me...	I act toward them...

2. How do you usually respond to people who blindly trust?

3. How do you usually respond to people who passively trust?

4. How do you usually respond to people who aggressively trust?

5. How do you think observing these patterns will help you to change?

6. What motivates you to change?

7. Are there any "wrong" motives? If so, what are they and how do they affect people?

8. How would you rate your own prognosis for change?

Learning to Trust
Perceptively

WE CAN TALK about global concepts like emotional healing, growth, and perceptive trust all day... and not
change one bit. These abstractions provide a useful framework,
but real change occurs in thousands of specific, individual
choices we face every day.

For years, many of us couldn't even *see* the choices. We had
a distorted perception of ourselves and others. We may have
confused trust with manipulation, isolation with safety, and
power over people with love for them. We've been so sub-
merged in our own misperceptions that we haven't known
what we wanted or needed. When asked a legitimate question
about our needs, we often didn't have a clue how to answer.

Jesus encountered such a man, one who had been incapaci-
tated for many years—perhaps someone much like ourselves.
We can read the story in the fifth chapter of the Gospel of
John. In Jerusalem by the sheep gate, "a multitude" of sick,
blind, lame, and paralyzed people waited for the waters of
Bethesda pool to be stirred by an angel of the Lord. Whoever
entered first was immediately healed of any disease. In this
mass of sick and needy people, Jesus approached one man who
had been sick for thirty-eight years.

"When Jesus saw him lying there, and knew that he had already been a long time in that condition, he said to him, 'Do you wish to get well?'" (Jn 5:6).

How would you expect this man to answer? "Sure!" or "You bet!" But he had been in the same condition for so long, with so little hope, that he had lost sight of his goal. He offered only an excuse to Jesus' question: "Sir, I have no man to put me into the pool when the water is stirred up, but while I am coming, another steps down before me" (Jn 5:7).

Perhaps this invalid was afraid of what life would be like if he were well. He'd have to be responsible. He would no longer have a ready excuse for his choices. He'd have to relate to people far differently. This man had forgotten his goal of wholeness. But Jesus didn't forget. Not even bothering to address the man's excuse, the Lord commanded him, "'Arise, take up your pallet, and walk.' And immediately the man became well" (Jn 5:8-9a).

Our merciful and compassionate Father doesn't abandon us. We may feel hopeless and helpless, but God intervenes. Even when we see no rhyme or reason in the circumstances in our lives, he is by our side. The man at the pool perceived life as a contest against other sick people to reach the healing waters first. Feeling forced to rely on his own meager strength, he had lost hope. But the Lord knew his needs from afar and offered a solution different from any he had considered.

God's answer for us may be long in coming and arrive in some unexpected way. A single mother may despair over losing her job, only to be led to a new company where the people care more about her. Another woman in the same predicament may fervently pray, only to end up in another painful work experience where no one values her contribution.

In his sovereignty, God leads some of us *out* of hurtful situations and others of us *through* them. We need to trust in him not so much for relief as for guidance and strength to grow in whatever soil he plants us. Our circumstances are never accidental. Knowing that God is at work in our behalf, our task is to listen and to cooperate.

MAKING MID-COURSE CORRECTIONS

As pointed out in the last chapter, admitting our need is the first step to help and healing. It is only the first step, but many of us never take it. Fear or pride, shame or defiance, bitterness or numbness—something keeps us from getting started. When we do realize something must change, we gather up our courage and take that step. Admitting our need begins our long journey of learning to trust perceptively.

What can we expect? The developmental process which may have been sidetracked during our childhood now needs to be reconstructed. The foundational elements of identity and autonomy were most likely built crooked or full of gaping holes. But we're no longer newborns starting out with no baggage. We're making a major mid-course correction, a process which requires a safe place where we can learn to trust and grow in our autonomy and identity.

As we learn to perceptively trust some people and not others, we also learn to trust our own judgment. We may have avoided all but the safest conclusions in the past because of our shame and self-doubt. Or perhaps we made decisions readily—even compulsively—out of defiance. True autonomy falls into neither of these extremes. It is quiet self-confidence. Certainly, autonomy involves risks, but the risks are not threatening to our deepest securities if we feel safe. If we fail, we can take responsibility and learn from our mistakes.

The freedom to make decisions and the willingness to take responsibility for those decisions form the basis for our identity. We find our ultimate security in Christ: loved, forgiven, and accepted because of his grace. We are related to God as members of his family. As a loving and attentive Father, he has given each of us gifts, talents, and abilities to develop and use. He even provides us with unique opportunities to best use these talents.

The drives and defenses each of us develops in our mistrust can be refocused and used to help us heal and grow. The energy used to please people or dominate them can be directed toward healthier decisions. The perception we have of others can be channeled into formulating clear goals and specific steps toward those goals. In fact, God delights in transforming negatives into positives.

What about the issue of safety? The problem is, most of us wouldn't know a safe place if it bit us! People accustomed to blind trust consider even dangerous characters safe. Passive and aggressive people distrust even the most trustworthy souls. We long for safety, we crave it, but we seem to have built-in barriers against it.

Our desperation, however, leads us to take a chance, to listen to a friend who says, "Come with me to the fellowship group I attend." Or, "Why don't you call this counselor? I hear she is really good. I bet she can help you."

Even when we muster the courage to make that first call or attend that first meeting or appointment, many of us feel deeply disappointed. We expected to become well—or at least a whole lot better! It takes us a while to realize that we need a "place called home" to promote our healing process rather than a "meeting pill" to get rid of our problems.

The first place we find may not be the one that best meets our needs. We may find it necessary to keep looking a while longer until we discover one we feel good about. We must take care, however, that we don't use uncomfortable feelings as an excuse to bounce from one counselor or group to another. Surfacing and grieving wounds, making hard decisions, and learning to relate to others differently will always be uncomfortable but necessary.

A nurturing environment offers the opportunity to be more honest with ourselves, about ourselves. We can begin to see patterns of mistrust, powerlessness or the acquisition of power, and repressed emotions. We can begin to perceive the way others have controlled us, as well as our attempts to control them through giving in, getting away, fixing their problems, or using intimidation. Growing perception allows us to recognize our thought processes, our defenses against being hurt, our drive to get approval and prestige, and the painful consequences of our behavior and our vulnerability to others.

A FIRM FOUNDATION

We all need a firm foundation on which to build—or rebuild—our lives. Four necessary building blocks are comfort, courage, clear goals, and confrontation.

Comfort. Comfort comes from feeling understood by empathetic people, especially those who have been through the same process. They can comfort others because they have been comforted. They don't dish out cheap advice. Their goal is not to solve our problems quickly so they'll feel better about themselves. Safe people are understanding, patient, and kind.

A safe place may be a fellowship group, or a counselor, or a friend, or a family, or even a church. When we find a place of safety, we can feel free enough to talk openly about our deepest fears and shame. We can finally experience the hurts and joys we have so long ignored. We can be ourselves without trying to impress others or hide from them. Sometimes people ask, "Pat, what is a safe place? What do you mean? I'm not sure I've ever been in one."

Good question! A safe place is where:

- You can be yourself.
- You have permission to feel.
- You can be wrong.
- You can be honest.
- Others will be honest with you.
- Others won't try to fix your problems.
- Others let you be responsible for yourself.
- You don't have to talk if you don't want to.

- Confidentiality will be honored.
- You will be loved, accepted, and forgiven.
- People will be honest with you.

We won't find any perfectly safe place until we reach heaven, of course. But as we experience relative safety in nurturing, honest human relationships, our perception of reality will sharpen. We can increasingly face the truth about ourselves, others, and God. Some of that truth will be quite comforting; some will feel like hell; much will fall somewhere in between.

Courage. My children enjoy watching *Rescue 911*, a weekly television program about paramedics and police who respond to real-life emergencies. Each show depicts four incidents of narrow escapes and close calls in which the rescuers demonstrate incredible skill and bravery. In the face of danger, the victims also exhibit exceptional courage, often a vital ingredient in the rescue.

Most people who work through emotional healing seldom make it to television dramas or talk shows. Yet each one of us needs tremendous personal courage to face the pain we've tried to escape, to experience the grueling grief process, and to learn to make hard decisions even in the face of ridicule, disdain, complacency, and misunderstanding. The struggle to address the internal mechanisms of guilt, shame, and self-hatred usually remains a lonely and quiet one. Over and over again, I marvel at the bravery of men and women who grieve, forgive, and take responsibility—one day at a time.

Clear goals. Several people who were taking part in a group discussion about growth and change mentioned a number of helpful tools that can help us to grow and change. We can read, be honest, listen, speak truth to a spouse or boss, do something fun, talk to a friend, forgive an offender, pay bills on time, and on and on. One woman had been very quiet through this whole discussion. At this point she leaned back in her chair and almost gasped, "I can't do all that! This is just my third week of reading about this stuff!"

We assured her that no one expects her to do all of these at once. They merely define a target for which to aim. We need clear goals in our current situations, wherever we happen to be in the healing process at a particular time. We can easily feel overwhelmed with all we need to acknowledge, grieve, say, and do. The more objective and realistic our goals, the greater our likelihood of achieving them.

We especially need to keep our goals focused on things we can control: *our* behavior, *our* decisions, *our* responsibility. We cannot control others. We need to let them make their own choices. Ultimately, our goal must be to speak the truth to others in love, not to control their responses.

All of us have goals, but we often base them on false expectations. We may try to act a certain way to get others to be nice to us. We may avoid conflict because we're afraid of being hurt. When our goal is to get others to meet our needs, our expectations are false. Our goals may be clear, but still misguided. If so, they will only lead to more blindness when met and reinforced.

Fran had been seeing Russ for counseling to get help with her marriage to Mark, who could be alternately charming and vicious. Sometimes, Fran would tell Russ about recent events, other times they talked about her childhood. Fran displayed classic blind trust. She wanted to please; she wanted to avoid conflict; she wanted to trust Mark because trusting him made her feel safer. As the counseling progressed, Fran expressed surprise every time Mark turned into Mr. Hyde. "I just can't believe he would treat me like that!"

After Fran once again described her husband's most recent tirade and expressed her usual disbelief, Russ paused. Then he looked intently at her and asked, "Fran, why are you surprised?"

"What do you mean?"

"I mean, why are you surprised that Mark acted that way?" Russ repeated.

Fran sat quietly for a while. She couldn't understand Russ's question—but she knew it was probably important! Finally, she spoke. "I guess I shouldn't be surprised, should I? I mean, he's really pretty consistent, isn't he?"

"Consistent enough," Russ answered. They then talked about Fran's persistent but false expectation—her hopeless hope—that Mark would magically change and never treat her harshly again. Her surprise at each point clearly revealed this false expectation which kept her locked into blindly trusting Mark. But now, this long-awaited vision had been shattered by a flash of reality. Russ comforted her as she wept.

"I feel so stupid!" Fran said disgustedly. "How could I be so blind for so long?"

"Don't be too hard on yourself, Fran," Russ encouraged. "A lot of people don't see reality as quickly as you have. And some never do."

Clarity in goals and expectations is tied directly to trust. As we feel safer around trustworthy people and as our self-confidence grows, we will be less susceptible to the pressures of pleasing people, giving in, getting away, or dominating others. These unhealthy behaviors—and the cloud of thoughts and feelings which envelop them—actually became goals in themselves, designed to protect and control.

Safety and confidence impart a healthy independence from these oppressive purposes. We learn to discern what the Lord wants instead of only what keeps people from criticizing us. We learn to embrace godly values, instead of thirsting for power over people or wanting just to be left alone.

Consider some examples of manipulative goals restated as healthy and helpful goals:

- *Get Jim to love me:* Be honest with Jim about our relationship and my hopes.
- *Get Sarah to listen to me:* Ask Sarah to listen to me.

- *Get Dad to stop yelling:* Tell Dad how his yelling makes me feel and ask him to stop.

- *Get Phil to quit drinking and go home:* Confront Phil about the effects of his drinking. If he doesn't respond, ask others to join in intervention.

- *Get Sally to be nice to me:* Speak kind words to Sally.

- *Get Mom to stop butting into my life:* Be honest with Mom; tell her "we need to communicate less often for a while because I need some space to make my own choices."

Pam described her painful relationship with her thirty-year-old son, Van. Their communication had been strained for years. She had been much too controlling when he was young, and even though she was doing better now, Van still resented her attempts to communicate with him. As Pam described the most recent event, she looked saddened and shaken by his anger.

I asked her, "What is your goal in that relationship?"

Pam replied to my question with a question of her own. "Huh?"

"What do you want from Van?" I repeated.

"Well, I guess I want him to care about me."

"OK," I answered. "That's your goal for him, but what's your goal for yourself?"

"For me? Well, I want to, uh, I don't know."

We talked about her inability to control Van and her responsibility to control herself in order to make good decisions about how to approach their relationship. That led us to specific goals. For our next time together, I asked Pam to complete these statements:

The situation is _____.

I normally respond _____.

I feel _____.

I want _____.

I will _____.

I expect _____.

I need _____.

I can trust in _____ to _____.

I shouldn't trust _____ to _____.

These statements helped Pam clarify her feelings, desires, and responsibilities. Then she could set specific goals regarding whether to communicate with Van, how much to say, how to listen, and when to say it. She was finally able to make progress without repeatedly hitting her head against a brick wall.

Confrontation. The fourth building block certainly requires courage, but it doesn't feel very safe or comfortable. Very few people actually enjoy confrontation. We usually think of someone yelling at us, pointing a finger in our faces, and accusing us of shameful acts—not necessarily speaking the truth in love.

Our ability to receive confrontation provides a sure test of our growing identity and autonomy. Many of us respond to even the slightest criticisms very defensively. As our sense of safety and security grow, however, we become better at accepting input without being sensitive. Some people confront us because they genuinely want to help us; others want to hurt us. As we become more secure, we will learn how to find the kernel of truth in any confrontation and learn from it.

Most of us find confronting someone who has hurt us to be a difficult and threatening task. When we come face-to-face with that individual, any number of misfires may occur. We may become confused. We may shut down emotionally or become violently angry. We may move toward resolution too quickly without being honest about the facts. We may hold on to bitterness and revenge instead of making progress in the relationship.

Confrontation comes in all sizes. It could be a minor correction spoken after a one-time verbal wound: "That hurt my feelings; please don't say that again." But confrontation can also address our most deeply rooted emotional issues. The following principles can help you make it through the mine field of working through interpersonal difficulties. Obviously, less serious incidents won't require as much preparation and careful progress as more painful ones. It is wise, however, to be over-prepared instead of ill-prepared.[1]

1. Be prepared. You would do well to apply the Boy Scout motto to your readiness to confront others. Preparation allows you to be more in control of your thoughts and behavior. You can more clearly determine what you really want in a relationship, and how confrontation could help you move toward that goal.

You may feel that if you have the courage to speak the truth, the other person ought to immediately repent in sackcloth and ashes. (Don't hold your breath!) On the other hand, you may fear that nothing will ever change. You may feel locked in a hopeless, shame-based relationship. That expectation is equally unrealistic because it denies your right to make healthy choices, as well as God's power to change lives.

Preparation involves knowing how you usually respond in similar situations. One man typically becomes fierce and intimidating out of fear of losing control. A high school student makes flip, sarcastic remarks to prove she's not affected. A woman becomes emotionally paralyzed and acquiesces to whatever the other person wants. If you know you tend to dominate, escape, or rationalize, you stand a much better chance of resisting that tendency.

Human beings often suffer from a severe case of tunnel vision. We don't see our own behavior and perceptions very well at all. You could prepare by seeking wise, objective input from a trusted friend, professional counselor, pastor, or in some cases, a lawyer. You need someone who can give you the feedback you need to set your course properly. When the person you need to confront is particularly hostile or intransigent, or when legal action is contemplated, you may need the active involvement of a third person in the confrontation itself.

Another aspect of being prepared involves anticipating the possible responses of the other person. Even if you think you can predict exactly how an individual will react, you may be surprised. You would be wise to consider a few "what ifs" and think through how you might respond.

2. *Major on the majors.* You may be able to enumerate hundreds of offenses which have hurt or bothered you, but such an exhaustive list would merely weaken your point. Narrow down your grievances until only a few remain. If more than a few are truly significant, choose the most important ones to discuss during the first meeting. If these are successfully resolved, the others can be addressed at a later meeting.

3. *You set the agenda.* To arrange the meeting, you could say something like, "I'd like to talk to you about our relationship. Can you meet me at ten o'clock Saturday morning?" Don't get pulled into a discussion about the issues at that point. Stay in control. Say, "I don't want to discuss it right now. We can talk at length on Saturday."

When the meeting begins, don't be vague about the topic of conversation. Even though your stomach may be tied in knots and your mind racing, state clearly what you see as the problem and communicate your desire to reach some resolution. Usually, the person you're confronting is at least as nervous as you are. And that person hasn't prepared like you have!

Those being confronted may use whatever manipulative techniques they've used on you before: self-pity, anger, yelling, silence, blaming you for the problem, accepting all the blame just to end the meeting, and so on. They'll probably try to get you off track and bring up other problems. Many people become confused and flustered at this point. I recommend taking a written agenda to the meeting with you. Whenever you need to refocus your thoughts, pull out the sheet and keep following your plan.

Obviously you want to be a good listener during this meeting, too. You may learn some things about yourself or the other person you never knew before. Passive people need to focus on being strong and resolute. Aggressive people need to be quiet and listen more.

4. Clarify points. One of the most effective ways to confront people is to "hold up a mirror," repeating what they've said or describing what they've done. Sometimes I will say, "This is what I hear you saying...." Then I'll try to repeat or rephrase what the person has just told me or the group. People often feel understood and gratified that someone else can articulate what they're feeling or thinking. Sometimes the person who is mirrored will say, "No, that's not it at all!" Perhaps we misunderstood, but perhaps the person is not objective enough to see the reality of his or her own statements. Either way, mirroring can lead to more discussion and understanding.

5. Stay in control of yourself. Be aware of your feelings of hurt, fear, confusion, guilt, and anger as the discussion progresses. Notice your body language. Are you slumping in the chair as the other person blames you for every problem the two of you ever had? Sit up! Are you averting your eyes because you fear condemnation and venomous looks? Be strong! Look that person in the eye and speak the truth. Are you leaning forward, interrupting, yelling? Calm down; sit back; apologize and listen.

6. Don't expect instant repentance. We are foolish to think most people will say, "You're exactly right. I have acted very badly and I am truly sorry. Please forgive me. How can I make it up to you?" It happens, but not very often. More often, they defensively react to being confronted—no matter whether the specific issues are simple or complex, relatively mild or serious, short-term or long-term. Give them time to reflect, pray, and think about their response. Schedule another appointment a few days later.

7. Now what? In any relationship, the course of action for each person depends on how the other responds. That sequence may be simple in the case of a black-or-white reaction. Perhaps an emotionally wounded woman slams her ex-boyfriend, "You're a jerk! I never did anything wrong!" Or she might say, "I'm sorry. What can I do to rebuild trust?"

Most responses to confrontation fall in between these extremes. A husband may agree he's hurt you, but still blame you for most of the problem. A good friend may use self-pity to get you to feel sorry for her and back off. Your father may say he's willing to change, but after multiple confrontations, no change has happened. Dad still says, "You don't understand. I'm really trying. Give me one more chance." (Which is what you've already done thirty-seven times before.) If you finally draw the line and set limits and expectations, he may try to make you feel so much guilt—or you may feel it on your own—that you believe you should give in—just one more time.

However people respond when confronted, you need to forgive them. Even if they don't ask for forgiveness, even if they will hurt you again, even if you don't want to forgive, you still need to forgive. The choice is unilateral. We are to forgive because it honors the Lord and frees us from the bitterness and bondage of seeking revenge.

No one said forgiveness is easy. It's not. But don't be confused: Forgiving doesn't mean you have to give in to someone's manipulation. It doesn't mean you have to blindly trust that person again. It doesn't mean you suddenly feel happy and carefree. Reconciliation is based on trust, and trust must be proven over time. Even if both parties want to reconcile, it doesn't happen instantly. The commitment to reconcile can happen in a moment, but the building of understanding, respect, and trust takes time.

When you do forgive, you come to grips with the reality of

your loss. True forgiveness necessarily involves grief. Especially if people are belligerent and manipulative, and even if they say they're willing to change but won't, you can recognize that you did all you could do. You talked, you spoke the truth in love, you forgave, you offered to build a relationship based on the strong foundation of mutual trust. If someone refuses, you can know you've done your best. In a situation just like this, a friend of mine was asked how he felt when his sister refused his offer of reconciliation. "Strong and sad," he said, "strong and sad."

8. Be strong. After a confrontation, you may be especially vulnerable to the elation of success or the despondency of failure. Either way, you may be tempted to let your guard down and slide back into the same old relationship rut. You let people treat you the same old ways without confronting them. You see a flash of change and excitedly think, "It's all over! They'll never treat me that way again!" And then you're devastated when they soon slip into the same pattern.

With all of the repressed anger of so many wounded years having now found a vent, you may be more furious than ever. Even if the other person wants to reconcile, now the problem may be you! You may refuse to give an inch. Or perhaps the confrontation has taken all the punch out of you. You feel emotionally drained, discouraged, and depressed.

Just as you needed a wise friend at the beginning of the process, that same friend is needed at the end to remind you to be strong, to forgive, and to make wise choices. And through it all, remember that this process can be accomplished best by depending on the Lord. He is the one who is ultimately trustworthy even when everyone else fails.

RISKY BUSINESS

Trust always involves some risk. We can't guarantee how the other person will respond. We can't even guarantee how God will respond, but we can be sure his ways are good and right.

Many people seem just as inscrutable as God, but our negative suspicions may be fully warranted.

The relationship may be between family members who have been embittered, distant, or only mildly offended. It may concern someone within your church family, or a business associate, or your next-door neighbor. Whether a relationship has just begun, is being built, or needs restoration after a break of trust, we need to be careful as we try to develop greater trust. We need to exercise controlled risk.

The principle of *controlled risk* means that we observe trustworthy behavior before we impart trust. As we have seen, accurately perceiving the behavior of others is not as easy as it sounds. Some of us can be blind to obvious, negative characteristics. Perhaps their lives reflect a clear pattern of deceit or laziness, backed up by a history of broken confidences. Others of us can be so guarded and suspicious that we refuse to take even the slightest risk with the most trustworthy person.

Perhaps we need to observe our own powers of observation before we attempt any assessment of other people. We would find it very helpful to solicit objective input from others in this regard. We may not want to hear what they say, but we're foolish if we don't at least consider the evaluations of mature people.

Distorted perceptions may lead us to all-or-nothing thinking. We might see someone as either completely trustworthy or not trustworthy at all, whereas most people can be trusted to do some things sometimes. I do recall one woman talking about her irresponsible, deceitful husband by saying, "If his mouth is open, he's lying!" That couple really needed to work on their trust relationship! We need to weigh the evidence, determine the other person's commitment to follow through on an agreement, possibly negotiate an acceptable risk for us, then move ahead.

This scenario happens in the business world every day. For example, a sales representative offers to sell a product to a company buyer for a certain price. The buyer must determine if the product's quality and the benefits to the company justify the expenditure. They talk, they negotiate, they make adjustments. Then the buyer decides whether or not to purchase this particular product.

Family life also involves this same process of weighing the evidence, determining the other person's commitment to follow through, and negotiating an acceptable risk. For example, a teenager asks her parents if she can spend the night with a friend, attend the school dance, and then go to a carnival the next day.

"Do you remember the last time you spent the night with someone?" Becky's dad asks her. "You stayed up until three o'clock in the morning. You were grumpy for three days and you didn't want to go on a hike with the rest of us."

"Yeah, I know. That won't happen this time," Becky insists.

Dad wants some specifics. "OK, I'm glad you understand that it was difficult for all of us last time. What will you do to make this time different?"

"I'll go to bed by 11:30, and I'll be sure to rest the next day when I get tired."

Dad wants to clarify the consequences. "And what if the same thing happens again? What do you think should happen?"

"I guess I shouldn't be allowed to go over to spend the night with anyone for a week," Becky answered.

"*Three* weeks," her dad counters.

"*Three weeks!* That's too long, Dad!"

"Three weeks and you can go tonight."

Becky realizes this is his final offer. "OK, it's a deal. You can count on me, Dad!"

Her parents are taking a controlled risk.

TRUTH OR CONSEQUENCES

After taking a controlled risk, the next step in building trust is continued objectivity. Look for the validation or the abrogation of the trust you've extended to someone. If your trust is confirmed, you can continue to build by risking again. If not, appropriate consequences should ensue.

In cases where trust has been violated, consequences need to be spelled out clearly, as in Becky's case. Many repercussions naturally result from certain actions: we don't go back to a doctor who rushed through our examination; we avoid shopping at a grocery store that consistently overcharges; we don't confide in a friend who gossiped about us. We may need to tell the person that the broken confidence has damaged the relationship, damage which can be mended only through honest communication. That painful process is consequence enough for most people!

Consequences provide checks and balances. They also hold out an opportunity to make mid-course corrections, to drop back a little, to reevaluate, and to let others prove their trustworthiness before we take another step forward.

In severely broken relationships, it is advisable to invite a third party to mediate and enforce the consequences. The two principal parties may despise and distrust each other so much that they find it impossible to make progress on their own. A trusted friend may help, but a peer is often seen as siding with one or the other. Usually, someone outside the circle of close friendships works best: a counselor, elder, pastor, or lawyer. Mediators can diffuse the anger between the two combatants, clarify volatile issues, and establish realistic objectives. They can also provide objective input so that each person knows what he or she needs to restore and build trust.

The history of some relationships revolves around deceit. Repeated assurances have gone unfulfilled. The only proof we see is that we should not trust them at all. In these cases, it is wise to state our perceptions clearly. If the person asks for "one more chance," we can give them that chance if we choose to, but the test case should be one that carries low risks for us.

One man asked his son to call him once a week. A woman asked her husband to come home after work every day and to stay with the family over the weekend. If he would do this for a month, perhaps they could take the next step. Building trust may have to begin on the most mundane and functional level, with little risk of personal and emotional issues such as reputation, sexual relations, finances, or public commitment. If the person validates this basic level of trust, we can move on. If not, clearly outlined consequences must be enforced.

In the process of starting, building, or restoring trust, we need not—and should not—speak out everything that comes to mind. An important element in regulating the level of risk is controlling the content of our communication. We say only what is helpful at that moment.

The apostle Paul referred to this principle when he instructed the believers at Ephesus: "Let no unwholesome word proceed from your mouth, but only such a word as is good for edification according to the need of the moment, that it may give grace to those who hear" (Eph 4:29). And to the Colossians: "Let your speech always be with grace, seasoned, as it were, with salt, so that you may know how you should respond to each person" (Col 4:6).

It may not be wise to tell an employer we feel hurt by a business decision. He may not care how we feel, and we may appear disloyal. We shouldn't tell a child how bitter we feel toward an unfaithful spouse. The child needs some information, but reassurance and comfort most of all. Too much information can easily damage an immature person. And we don't need to tell a spouse everything we've ever thought and felt as part of an atomic-bomb conversation. Venting negative emotions may spell relief to us, but usually damages the relationship.

In summary: control the level of risk, not foolishly trusting unproven people, nor being too cautious, either. Go step by step. The long journey of building a relationship requires both determination and patience.

NO EASY FORMULAS

A man attending one of my seminars asked, "We've talked about grieving the past, and we've talked about responding well today. Which one should I focus on?"

The answer, of course, is both. We need to address the wounds and compulsive behaviors of the past because they color virtually every thought, relationship, and behavior we have today. These hurts need to be grieved. These malfunctioning behaviors need to be understood and replaced. But the Scriptures never grant us permission to behave however we want while we do so. We are commanded to be sober, to act righteously, to forgive, to love, to serve, and to give. God always holds us responsible for today's actions.

Our expectations, however, focus on progress, not perfection. All of us, even those from the most stable, loving homes, are fallen people in the process of being sanctified by God's grace. John Bunyon wrote of *Pilgrim's Progress,* not *Pilgrim's Perfection.* His classic work describes the many difficulties, temptations, and pitfalls in our walk with God. For many of us, this pilgrimage feels like a long hike through mud and muck. After a while, each step evokes pain. We feel so tired. If our concentration lapses just a moment, we fall. When we do fall, we can lie in the mud, or get up and keep trudging. Thousands of little decisions, little steps, mark our path.

As long and slow and painful as our journey seems at times, progress seems a mystery. The Lord brings refreshment from others who encourage us. He gives us strength when we think we can't take another step. He comforts us by his people, his Word, and his Spirit when we fall. We are not alone. God is always at work in us—even when we think he's taken a vacation!

Perhaps you expected a formula to help you learn how to trust perceptively. We can identify principles of progress and certain basic necessities, but no formulas. Perceptive trust is not primarily something you do. Throughout this healing process, our decisions and activities draw their strength and their meaning from the intangibles of feeling safe, sensing others' good will, and taking risks and seeing if these risks are validated. Checkpoints help us know if we're making progress; reflection questions help us make good decisions; and accountability helps assure our follow-through. But trusting in others and trusting ourselves cannot be reduced to an outline.

Why do so many of us gravitate toward formulas in our relationships? With them, we feel safer. We feel in control. But defining life in terms of rules does not equal trust. Discipline is a virtue if it enhances our relationships with God and others. As the primary architect of meaning in our lives, however, discipline leaves us cold, dry, rigid, and lonely.

Placing our trust in others will inevitably lead to disappointments. Some people may not listen, love, or even try to understand us. But the risks are well worth taking. Perceptive trust yields more wisdom, richness in relationships, honor, integrity, and real life. Loving and being loved prove infinitely deeper and more meaningful than checking off accomplishments on a mental to-do list or avoiding interaction out of fear. The risks are real, but so are the rewards.

❖ ❖ ❖

Take Time to Reflect

1. What would you like to see changed in your most important relationships?

2. What could you realistically do to stimulate those changes?

3. In what ways do you look to others to give you a sense of comfort? Are you too quick to take hope? Why or why not?

4. What might you say if you were to confront your own weaknesses?

5. Complete these two sentences: Some of the things I can do to show my courage in building healthy relationships include: _____.

   A goal I can realistically achieve in my relationships is: _____

   _____.

6. What could you do to prevent change from happening in your relationships?

7. You can't control others, but you can control yourself. In what ways could you better control your interactions with others?

8. Name some unrealistic goals you've had in the past. How have these affected you and your relationships?

9. In what personal situation do you need to clearly define the goals you want to work toward?

10. What changes in your behavior and communications will you attempt to make in that relationship? Complete the following chart.

    The situation is: _____.

    I normally respond: _____.

    I feel: _____.

    I want: _____.

    I will: _____.

I expect: _____.

I need: _____.

I can trust in _____ to _____.

I shouldn't trust _____ to _____.

12

Hobbled by Unbelief

*A*S YOU PROBABLY KNOW through painful experience, believers are not immune to struggles of faith. We've read the stories, heard the sermons, and prayed the prayers, but we still feel torn by inner conflict and ambivalence. We believe, yet we doubt.

Our spiritual condition may be exemplified by the man who approached Jesus with his demon-possessed son, a young boy who was convulsing and frothing at the mouth. "And he asked his father, 'How long has this been happening to him?' And he said, 'From childhood. And it has often thrown him both into the fire and into the water to destroy him. But if you can do anything, take pity on us and help us!' And Jesus said to him, '"If you can!" All things are possible to him who believes.' Immediately the boy's father cried out and began saying, 'I do believe; help my unbelief'" (Mk 9:21-24).

I believe, but I don't. Help me! Haven't you felt that way on many occasions? I certainly have. The mistrust which plagues human relationships also afflicts our relationship with God. In fact, our relationship with God is usually a reflection of the mistrust we've developed with our parents. Their attitudes and actions modeled God's authority for us. If they smothered us, we probably believe that we have to do everything God could possibly expect of us. If they were harsh, we may find it difficult to believe in God's lovingkindness. If they were aloof, we're likely to believe that God isn't interested in us either.

God alone is totally trustworthy. We can count on him to accomplish *his* purposes, but we often want God to accomplish *our* purposes instead. We think we know what we want, and we believe what we want is best. But God transcends and defies our all-too-human logic. The Almighty doesn't bow to our wishes; we bow to his. This proposition would be threatening —and unsafe—if God were mean-spirited, but we call him both Master and Father. The one who rules is also the one who cares, protects, and provides.

The Scriptures speak eloquently of God's provision of love (1 Jn 4:10), acceptance (Col 1:19-22), and forgiveness (Col 2:13-14). He gives wisdom to those who ask in faith (Jas 1:5-8) and strength to follow his will (Is 41:10). We are encouraged to ask God to provide our specific temporal needs (Mt 6:33), but often our requests are misguided (Jas 4:1-3).

Whatever the outcome of putting our trust in God, we can at all times go to the center of our faith, the unchangeable nature of God's goodness and power. The death and resurrection of Christ most vividly demonstrated the divine character. In this one wrenching act of self-sacrifice, God offered forgiveness. He reached out to us and communicated both his great love and his great power.

Can we not then believe God for even the little things in life? "He who did not spare his own Son, but delivered him up for us all, how will he not also with him freely give us all things?" (Rom 8:32). Whether God provides what we ask or not, our hope rests ultimately in his unchangeable nature. The essence of our trust is found in the awesome power of God coupled with his tender mercies.

USING GOD

All three types of trust and distrust attempt to use God to attain their perceived need of approval, distance, or success. People with blind trust busily serve God and expect him to reciprocate. After all, they've done so much for him, they deserve having God come through for them! Those who trust without question often feel very close to God, just as they feel close to other people with whom they're enmeshed. But they tend to be driven by guilt, fear, and shame, not the freedom of God's grace.

People with passive distrust have an innate fear of authority. They try to stay detached so that a powerful authority figure doesn't have access to hurt them. Perceiving God as the most threatening authority of all, they often feel distant from him. They may approach him when they're really needy, but they feel guilty, awkward, and all alone.

People with passive distrust may feel self-sufficient in some areas of strength, but they often feel helpless and hopeless. They may avoid any kind of religious experience, or they may go through the motions of worship, prayer, and Bible study. Either pathway feels lifeless and empty—just like most of their human relationships. While distancing themselves hurts, avoiding the threat of intimacy comforts.

If we don't feel safe with any human being, we often feel driven to find someone who is totally and ultimately safe. Christians who passively distrust often make God their safe place and develop a blind-trust relationship with him. By depending on the invisible Lord to meet their need for intimacy, they can continue to avoid the flesh-and-blood people in their lives. Their trust in God may seem good and right, but it is often magical and imaginary. Meanwhile, they may continue to slide past the Scriptures which admonish us to relate to people in healthy ways.

People with aggressive distrust can be busier than anyone else in their church work and private spiritual lives, but their goals and motives usually differ. They serve not to please or to win love. They typically want to use their knowledge of the Bible, their ability to articulate doctrine, and their status as leaders to dominate others. Those who aggressively distrust may treat God like other authority figures and try to accomplish a lot to gain leverage.

MIRROR IMAGES

While our mistrust of God tends to be an exact replica of our relationship with our parents, it may also reflect an equal but opposite reaction. For example, Peggy is very passive in almost every relationship in her life, but she relates to God out of blind trust. She explained, "When I became a Christian, it's like all my latent hopes and desires to be loved and to feel close came to the surface and were focused on Jesus. You know the song, 'He's Everything to Me'? Well, I wanted him to be everything to me! For the first time in my life, I felt loved. It was wonderful."

Then Peggy's voice grew somber. "But it was awful. I became obsessed with doing everything perfectly to please God. I made up stupid rules of how much to read the Bible, how much to pray, how many times to go to church each week. But no matter how well I adhered to my rules, I still felt I needed to do more to please him. I'm confused. How can you feel so close to the Lord and feel so guilty, too?"

My own experience was similar at first, but later took a dramatic shift. When I became a Christian in college, my relationship with God showed the classic symptoms of blind trust so typical of my youth: eager to please, active in ministry, feeling close to him but also driven by fear and guilt... the whole bit. I trusted God to fix my every problem. When he didn't, I minimized, "Oh, it wasn't a big deal anyway."

Several years out of college, a number of traumatic events converged in my own life. My family, my boss, and several other people became very demanding or disappointed in me. I prayed. I mean, I really prayed! But the situation only worsened.

My conclusion: God had let me down. He wasn't trustworthy anymore. In my eyes, the deity went from lily white to some shade of gray. I still considered God to be omniscient, omnipresent, and omnipotent, but he certainly didn't care about me. Entering a passive-distrust phase, I no longer expected much from God—I just didn't want him to hurt me again. I continued to go through all the same motions. After all, I wanted to be a "good" Christian. But my life with God felt empty and meaningless. Occasionally, I would enjoy spurts of renewed closeness with the Lord, but would soon return to low tide.

MAKING UP THE RULES AS WE GO

Many of us have internalized fundamental misconceptions about our relationship with God. When these faulty perspectives are exposed, we can refute them with the truth. Unfortunately, these misconceptions lie hidden in our subconscious minds, unseen but powerful enough to affect every aspect of our lives.

Each of these false beliefs can usually be stated as an extreme of a biblical truth, skewed notions which can be substantiated from the Scriptures (if you're willing to twist interpretation and application a bit). Let's examine a few of them.

"God will protect you from all problems." Many Christians believe a slight variation of this falsehood: "God will protect you from *major* problems." Little ones are OK, but surely God doesn't want his children to hurt, does he? Apparently he does. Just ask Job, or Jeremiah, or the folks in Hebrews 11, or Paul, or countless other dedicated believers who suffered—and continue to suffer—for their faith. This type of blind trust eventually leads to deep disappointment and disillusionment.

Some modern evangelicals teach that the Christian life entails not only the protection of God from problems but also complete mastery over previously unbridled lusts and sinful behavior. For those who realize they cannot possibly live up to this perfect standard, this teaching can lead to intense self-condemnation, extreme guilt and shame, and eventually, a breakdown of faith. In *Knowing God*, J.I. Packer observes that this "cruel ministry" hinders our ability to forthrightly tackle our fleshly nature and encourages us to deny our faults because they threaten our status of "good Christians." He writes:

> What, basically, is wrong with this teaching? It is open to criticism from many angles. It fails to grasp New Testament teaching on sanctification and the Christian warfare. It does not understand the meaning of growth in grace. It does not understand the operations of indwelling sin. It confuses the Christian life on earth with the Christian life as it will be in heaven. It misconceives the psychology of Christian obedience (Spirit-prompted activity, not Spirit-prompted passivity). But the basic criticism must surely be that it loses sight of the method and purpose of grace.
>
> How does God in grace prosecute this purpose? Not by shielding us from assault by the world, the flesh, and the devil, nor by protecting us from burdensome and frustrating circumstances, nor yet by shielding us from troubles created by our own temperament and psychology; but rather by exposing us to all these things, so as to overwhelm us with a sense of our own inadequacy, and to drive us to cling to him more closely. This is the ultimate reason, from our standpoint, why God fills our lives with troubles and perplexities of one sort or another—it is to ensure that we shall learn to hold him fast.[1]

"God will fix any problem." We may position ourselves one notch down from ultimate and complete protection: God will at least right every wrong and meet every need. Indeed, our Father can and will meet many needs, but he wants us to depend on him alone. As members of a corrupt, fallen race, we suffer some irreparable problems as the consequences of sin— ours or that of others.

As a pitcher for the San Francisco Giants, Dave Dravecky was a big league star with a blazing fastball and a wicked curve. Then he learned he had cancer. After battling the disease for months, he went through surgery to remove cancerous tissue from his arm. More months of rigorous rehabilitation followed because Dave was determined to pitch again for the Giants. The hours of sweating over weights finally paid off when Dave Dravecky received a hero's welcome at Candlestick Park.

The public and private excitement evaporated when the doctors discovered more tumors. They recommended amputation. No choices remained. After a successful career and an amazing comeback, it was over.

If their source of livelihood and identity is suddenly shattered, many athletes become bitter over career-ending injuries. But not Dave Dravecky. Throughout the whole ordeal of diagnosis, surgery, rehabilitation, relapse, and amputation, he knew his life was more than baseball.

God hadn't protected this man from huge problems and didn't let his amazing comeback last for long, but Dave knew his heavenly Father was strong and near to him in the midst of it all. Today, Dave Dravecky's books and speaking engagements inspire thousands to see that life's problems don't mean that God is evil or uncaring.

"God's peace eliminates unpleasant feelings." We love to read about God's peace in passages like this one in Philippians: "Be anxious for nothing, but in everything by prayer and supplication with thanksgiving let your requests be made known to God. And the peace of God, which surpasses all comprehension, shall guard your hearts and your minds in Christ Jesus" (Phil 4:6-7).

That kind of peace sounds so wonderful. But unpleasant feelings are not evils to be avoided at all costs. Hurt, anger, and sadness may stem from our own disobedience or from others' sins against us. Even so, such emotions are God-given signals to us. These flashing lights on our emotional dashboard tell us something is wrong under the hood and needs to be examined. God may also orchestrate circumstances in our lives to test our faith (Jas 1:2-4), deepen our dependence on him (Prv 3:5-6), or prune us for greater fruitfulness (Jn 15).

Our culture places a very high value on pleasant feelings. We can easily believe that unpleasant emotions somehow do not fall within the parameters of God's providential care. Yet the peace which he gives differs dramatically from the mere absence of hassles (Jn 14:27). And it does not preclude how we experience the feelings of others.

We often wish God would inspire someone to appreciate us, get off our backs, give us a raise or promotion, pat us on the back, or give us affection—but it doesn't happen. Instead, we feel taken for granted, condemned, ridiculed, and used. It hurts! We may not be able to identify the cause of our emotional pain. We may be experiencing the consequences of bad decisions; we may feel the effects of someone else's choice to do evil; but we may be in exactly the right place to learn about God's grace and strength.

In his insightful book *Trusting God,* Jerry Bridges observes that the sovereign Lord of all uses people—even those who care nothing about God or even hate God—to carry out his purposes in our lives.

How are we to respond when we find ourselves seemingly in the hands of someone else, when we desperately need a favorable decision or a favorable action on that person's part? Can we trust God that he can and will work in the heart of that individual to bring about his plan for us?

We can trust God. He does sovereignly intervene in the hearts of people so that they make decisions and carry out actions that accomplish his purpose for our lives. Yet God does this in such a way that these people make their decisions and carry out their plans by their own free and voluntary choices.[2]

We need to remember that the actions and decisions of others carry out *God's* purposes, not necessarily ours. Instead of "kicking against the goads" and wanting only relief from the hurt, we would do well to reflect, to listen, and to trust God to accomplish something different than we had planned.

"If I do enough for God, he'll give me what I want."
Many of us espouse a doctrine of grace but live a doctrine of
righteousness by works. We believe we can twist God's celestial
arm to give us what we want—perhaps love, success, riches, or
peace—if we do certain things for him. We may focus on our
devotional life, structuring it to achieve an acceptable level of
time or content. Or we may focus on service, administrative
work, or some other avenue of gaining leverage. But God will
not be bribed.

"God doesn't care about me; I'm on my own." One man
told me sadly, "If God really does care, I sure wish he'd let me
know about it." Like this hopeless person, many of us feel
abandoned by all authority, even God, and especially God. If
we stop to think about it, we can understand that mere human
beings have their own problems. We excuse them for not caring. But God? Why do we feel so far from him? Other people
seem to feel close; what about us? At times we feel much like
the psalmist:

How long, O Lord: Wilt thou forget me forever?
How long wilt thou hide thy face from me?
How long shall I take counsel in my soul,
Having sorrow in my heart all the day?
How long will my enemy be exalted over me?
Consider and answer me, O Lord, my God;
Enlighten my eyes, lest I sleep the sleep of death.

Psalm 13:1-3

"God caused your pain so he can use you to help others."
Some well-meaning but insensitive people encourage us by
pointing out that our pain has meaning. Someone who has
been deeply wounded needs understanding and comfort, not
opportunities to minister to others. We certainly want God to
use us to advance his kingdom, but first things first. We want
to be loved! Using our pain to help others seems cruel and
heartless of God. Perhaps later we can realize that our tragedy

can ultimately be used for good, but surely God is not so utilitarian to have that as the primary reason for suffering! Those who mourn need to be comforted, not challenged to greater effectiveness.

These and many other misconceptions can easily destroy love and sap the life and spontaneity out of our relationship with God. Consequently, many of us end up relating to God more as an employer rather than a loving Lord. We do things *for* him, but seldom *with* him. We see God's blessings as earnings for our labor rather than gifts. We feel motivated by guilt, shame, and fear rather than being empowered by the love of Christ. We look forward to another divine paycheck or bonus instead of enjoying a rich relationship with God the Father. We listen for orders rather than hearing words of love.

"COMFORT, COMFORT, MY PEOPLE"

Those of us who have been deeply wounded become absorbed in our pain and the entangled web of strained relationships and difficult situations. We construct elaborate defenses to protect us from more hurt, but these only keep us more isolated. And all the while, our deepest longing is to love and be loved; to know and be known.

The comfort, encouragement, strength, wisdom, and hope of knowing God surpasses all else in life, including wounds, bitterness, confusion, and emptiness. After Paul recounted all his prestige and status, he wrote that nothing could compare to intimacy with Christ: "But whatever things were gain to me, those things I have counted as loss for the sake of Christ. More than that, I count all things to be loss in view of the surpassing value of knowing Christ Jesus my Lord, for whom I have suffered the loss of all things, and count them but rubbish in order that I may gain Christ" (Phil 3:7-8).

We long for love, but our defenses keep us isolated. God wants to give each one of us the courage to begin removing the bricks, one by one. We often see the difficulties, drudgeries, and tragedies of life as hindrances, but God can use them to teach us both our neediness and his trustworthiness. Some have said that the human heart is so wayward that we won't trust in God until we have to. In fact, our problems force a dependence on God, the proper relationship between creature and Creator.

We won't necessarily learn the "hidden reason" for every event. Sometimes we can see that a job layoff ultimately led to a better work situation. A teenager's unruly behavior may have painful consequences, but these may lead to a genuine turn-around in his life. Often, however, we won't be able to see the physical, tangible, identifiable reason for the difficulty. We can be sure of only one thing: God wanted to produce dependence.

A couple of years ago, my wife went to the doctor for her annual physical. After her mother died of cancer several years earlier, she had been advised to schedule a checkup regularly "just to be safe." On this particular occasion, Joyce came home saying, "Everything looks fine. They'll call me about the lab report on the blood work." We were glad of the good news.

A few days later, the doctor called to say Joyce's red blood count was abnormally low. "It's probably just an error in the test or a temporary problem caused by a virus. Have you had a virus in the last few weeks?" he asked.

"No. No, I haven't," Joyce responded.

"Well, come in for some more blood work in two weeks. It should be normal by then," the doctor assured her.

Joyce went for the blood tests, feeling fairly confident the problem wouldn't surface again.

A few days later, the doctor called. "Mrs. Springle, I'm going to arrange an appointment with a hematologist. Your red count is still well below the normal range. When can you see him?"

Joyce's confidence evaporated in a flash. "I can see him any-time. Tomorrow would be fine." Then, summoning the courage to ask the obvious but dreaded question, "What do you think this could be?"

"I'm not sure. It could be the residual effect of a virus."

"But I haven't had a virus!" Joyce interrupted.

"Yes, I see," the doctor remembered. "Well, Mrs. Springle, it could be a number of things."

"Like cancer?"

"Yes, possibly lymphoma." After a pause, he said, "I'll schedule you with the specialist. We'll know for sure after that. Try not to worry."

Lymphoma. The word sounded like a death sentence. Joyce remembered her mother's long, painful ordeal of breast cancer, surgery, then a reappearance of cancer in her bones, then month after month of hopeless therapy, wanting to die, pain, loss of control, and finally death. I tried to comfort her as she cried. Objectivity about the range of possibilities seemed pretty hollow, so we just sat together. "Of all the things I dread the most, this is my worst nightmare," she sobbed.

A week that seemed like ten years passed before my wife's appointment with the hematologist. More tests, more waiting. Same result. He called, "Mrs. Springle, your red count is still abnormally low. Let's run a different test and see what we find." More uncertainty, which led to more wondering, fear, and doubt.

And more prayer. Joyce prayed as she never had before. She prayed that the blood count would return to normal. She prayed that she didn't have lymphoma. She prayed for strength to endure the worst. She prayed the doctor would call and tell her it was all a mistake.

More tests followed, but the hematologist said he was stumped. "Let's wait six months and see if there's any change."

Joyce felt relieved and more fearful at the same time. "If he doesn't see anything clearly, then I guess I don't need to worry. Surely, if he were concerned, he'd do something right away." But also, she thought, "What if I have lymphoma? In six months, it might be so advanced, I'll have no chance at all!"

The months passed slowly. Joyce tried to keep her mind off the next doctor visit, but the thought was always on the back burner. The day finally came with new waves of hopes and fears. More tests. More waiting.

"Mrs. Springle, your red count is at the same level as before.

We'll need to do more extensive tests this time. I don't feel comfortable with your blood count at this level."

He didn't feel comfortable! Joyce felt anything but comfortable about the doctor's uncertainty. His lack of clarity led to thoughts of the worst and more earnest prayer.

This next series of tests was designed to shed light on how the red blood count might be related to other medical factors. It showed the same low red count, but again proved inconclusive in pinpointing the cause.

The doctor suggested, "Why don't we wait a year and test it again? If your red count remains what it has been, we'll need to test your bone marrow."

By now Joyce had become accustomed to her constant companion: a vague but nagging anxiety. The uneasiness propelled her to focus on the Lord, to reflect on his character, and to be specific in her requests.

A year later, yet another battery of blood tests revealed the same blood count as before. When the doctor told her the results, he said, "Mrs. Springle, I don't know what to say. This must be your normal level since it hasn't varied over this time and you have no symptoms of sickness."

Over those past couple of years, Joyce had desperately wanted to hear the word "normal." It was spoken in a different context than expected, but she'd take it!

"All the fear, all the thoughts about dying of cancer, all the doctors' visits, just to find out that my normal red blood count is lower than most people's. Why did the Lord put us through this?" After she thought for a minute, Joyce answered her own question, "At least I've grown closer to the Lord than ever before."

IS GOD GOOD?

We easily ponder the greatness and sovereignty of God when we look up at the vast expanse of stars, but we find it difficult to accept life's persistent problems and occasional tragedies. In our confusion and hurt, we often ask, "Why?"

Human beings often exercise power out of fear and greed, to rule over others. God always wields his infinite power in the context of his infinite love. If our parents or other authority figures have been capricious, aloof, or condemning, we learned to doubt their intentions—for good reason. Our trust in God hinges on this vital issue: Do we believe that he is good and that he has our best interests at heart?

Jesus compared God's generosity to a loving father's desire to give good gifts to his children. In the parable of the prodigal son, he described how the father forgave his wayward son and generously reinstated him into the family. By contrasting God to selfish and rigid religious rulers, Jesus made clear the gentle, gracious, and protective nature of the Father. He can be trusted.

In *The God Who Hears,* W. Bingham Hunter emphatically states that our perception of God's goodness is essential to our faith.

> We cannot overemphasize the importance of the conviction that God's character is wholly good, gracious and compassionate. Why is this conviction so important? Because faith trusts in God rather than insisting on its own way. Such faith is certain that God always responds with goodness and wisdom when our prayers are consistent with God's will but are not based on specific promises in Scripture. This kind of faith, as Bishop B.F. Wescott said, results in "not so much the granting of a specific petition, which is assumed by the petitioner to be the way to the end desired, but the assurance that what is granted does most effectively lead to that end."[3]

Learning to listen. Most of us are so busy that we seldom take time to listen. We work, we watch, we play, but we don't often focus on others. We need to learn to listen to God, too. A trust relationship can't be developed if both parties aren't communicating and listening.

God communicates with us through his Word, his Spirit, and his people. We approach listening, however, from divergent angles. Those who blindly trust often hear more than God communicates. Susceptible to being misled, they must use caution and test "messages" to make sure they're from the Lord.

Most passive people hear very little, simply because they don't expect to hear from God. They're afraid to ask God for help. What if he says no? What if he doesn't come through? That would hurt too much. It's easier—and safer—not to ask at all. Those who passively distrust need the courage to hope and the courage to take the risk of listening. Aggressive people usually hear reflections of themselves. Their man-made god is interested in their success, power, and fame. They need meekness.

Of course, we all tend to hear what we want to hear—or what we're afraid to hear. We need wise, godly friends to give us honest feedback as we read the Bible and pray. Trusting God isn't easy for many people, but it is possible. God knows; God cares; God provides. Over the past several years, the Lord has been renewing my trust in him—not blind trust with all its baggage, but a clearer perception of his character, his grace, and my need for him.

SIMPLY TRUST AND OBEY?

Has anyone ever encouraged you to "put your trust in Jesus" or to "simply believe"? Certain aspects of our relationship with God are indeed clear and simple. He is the Creator, the sovereign Lord; we are needy, fallen people. God initiates; we respond.

But our relationship with God also carries elements of complexity. We may be confused about specific interpretations of biblical truth, as well as how to apply that truth in light of cultural complexities. If the Christian faith were truly simple, we wouldn't have hundreds of denominations thinking they have the corner on truth, and my Bible wouldn't be 1950 pages long!

Even a cursory reading of the Scriptures makes us aware of two worlds, the seen and the unseen. Most of our struggles have their roots in any of several sources: perhaps the consequences of our sins or the sins of others; God's testing, pruning, and refining; and spiritual conflict. These forces most often combine to wreak havoc in our lives.

In our woundedness, we tend to see only the visible and the tangible. We want solutions we can taste, feel, and see. But as Paul says, our real struggle deals not with the tangible, not with our parents, children, spouse, boss, or ourselves. "For our struggle is not against flesh and blood, but against the rulers, against the powers, against the world forces of this darkness, against the spiritual forces of wickedness in the heavenly places" (Eph 6:12).

The enemy of our souls is frightfully real, and he certainly does not have our best interests at heart. Satan wants to confuse our minds, twist our thoughts, deceive us about God's love and strength, and make us doubt our safe refuge in Christ.

As you consider your ability to trust God and clearly perceive his nature, be aware that unseen spiritual forces are always at work to prevent—or at least hinder—your growth. The enemy is strong and he does not play fair. But the Lord is far greater, "far above all rule and authority and power and dominion, and every name that is named, not only in this age, but also in the one to come" (Eph 1:21).

Much has been written about spiritual conflict. I encourage you to read, study, discuss, and believe. If you at least recognize the reality of the conflict, you can use greater discernment and faith in your struggle.

Paul encouraged the Corinthian believers to destroy every unbelief with divine weapons: "For though we walk in the flesh, we do not war according to the flesh, for the weapons of our warfare are not of the flesh, but divinely powerful for the destruction of fortresses. We are destroying speculations and every lofty thing raised up against the knowledge of God, and we are taking every thought captive to the obedience of Christ" (2 Cor 10:3-5). We need to come against our own misconceptions in the same way.

I can almost see some people in my fellowship group. After a discussion of what it means to trust God, several would look at me and say, "OK, all this sounds good, but how do I *experience* it?"

All growing relationships combine the two components of function and mystery. True communication begins with a realistic appraisal of the relationship, along with a willingness to discuss it and to take practical steps toward understanding and intimacy. But no communication will occur without the desire to know and be known.

God has placed in each of us a desire, a longing, even a desperate need to know and love him. We don't have to try to acquire this hunger; it's something we already have which needs to be awakened. Relationships can begin from the most halting and stammering start. Then they build as each person learns to communicate and to listen, to know and to be known. We only need to step out and pursue the Lord, knowing he longs to be known by us and certainly possesses adequate communication skills. As Hosea wrote, "So let us know, let us press on to know the Lord. His going forth is as certain as the dawn; and he will come to us like the rain, like the spring rain watering the earth" (Hos 6:3).

Relationships also involve an element of mystery. They go beyond the functional into the soulish aspect of relating. Knowing and being known awakens the spirit, and two people grow together through the intangibles of desire, love, nearness, understanding, forgiveness, and commitment.

Again, no easy formula exists. Real relationships cannot be quantified. We respond to the one who loved us first by disciplined pursuit. We begin with an open Bible and an open heart, allowing God to speak to us as we have the courage to speak and to listen.

❖ ❖ ❖

Take Time to Reflect

1. In what ways did your family relationships affect the way you view God (both positively and negatively)?

2. Can you recall a childhood experience in which you realized your parents were imperfect? What impact did that experience have on you?

3. What possible misconceptions do you have about God?

4. Name some of the ways God may want you to cooperate with him to bring healing to broken relationships.

5. What are some positive things you learned about God as a result of a particular relationship failure?

6. List some Scripture verses that speak strongly to you of the trustworthiness of God.

13

If You Can't Trust Yourself...

*I*N THE SUMMER before my senior year in college, my buddy, Graham, and I headed west from Georgia. We had saved enough money from our summer jobs to have a fling, one last month of freedom before another nine months of school and forty-five years of work ruined our lives.

Graham and I did it all. We hiked to the bottom of the Grand Canyon and back. Going down wasn't too tough, but coming back up—whew! We spent a week in Los Angeles and did the usual tourist stuff: Universal Studios, the beach, Olvera Street, La Brea Tar Pits, and on and on. The next week, we camped up the California coast following Route One. We body-surfed with the sea lions at Carpenteria and watched the waves at San Luis Obisbo glow at sunset with phosphorescent algae. That was quite a show for two Georgia boys!

A day or two later, Graham and I drove up to Big Sur. The spectacular surf beckoned so strongly that we could resist no longer. At the mouth of the Little Sur River, we parked the car, climbed down the cliffs, and headed for the ocean. As we crossed the sand, I noticed that the crash of the waves seemed especially loud. But then, bigger waves, better body-surfing, right? No problem! Once we reached the water line, I also noticed that the sand turned to rocks and the beach sloped off quite steeply.

I plunged into the water, swam through a couple of breakers, turned, and caught a good one. The ride was exhilarating—for about two seconds. Then the wave slammed me into the rocks on the steep bank of the beach. I was knocked almost senseless.

I stood up and tried to clear my brain. Then, a second later... bam! Another wave (can't we call a time-out?) slammed me into the rocks again. I crawled out of the surf and collapsed onto the sand.

I heard a voice above the din of the crashing waves. Graham yelled, "This is great, isn't it?"

What I wanted to say was... never mind.

Why hadn't I noticed the danger signals? Why had I rushed in like a fool? Why was my head ringing while my buddy feasted on the beauty of nature?

Failure and defeat can shake our self-confidence. Depending on the nature of the reversal, our apprehensions may be temporary or long-term, mild or intense. How does the ability to trust ourselves contribute to healthy relationships?

WHAT IS SELF-CONFIDENCE?

Many Christians misunderstand and malign self-confidence. "We shouldn't trust in ourselves," they say with conviction. "We should only trust in God!" Authentic self-confidence, however, involves a true appraisal of our strengths and weaknesses which is the opposite of ego-centered pride. Knowing our limitations does not equal shame; being confident in our abilities does not parallel pride.

As we discussed in chapter two, self-trust begins to develop in early childhood, after we learn to trust in others to protect us and provide us with the necessities of life. In a safe, nurturing environment, we begin to flap our fledgling wings and assert our autonomy—but only a little. We still depend on our caregivers to meet our basic needs. We also depend on trustworthy others to provide direction and limits in our new attempts to be separate.

This process of exercising independence in the context of trust relationships builds our self-confidence. We learn to believe in our ability to make decisions. We try and fail so often that we eventually learn to do something right. Think of a toddler who works to fit a block into a puzzle. She tries and tries until she gets it, then struts in triumph at her accomplishment.

But autonomy also means that we know our limitations. We learn that we can't do everything. This same toddler may try to climb a tree, but the lowest limb is six feet off the ground. She soon abandons her efforts.

One of my limitations is higher math. Since I breezed through all my high school math courses, I thought differential calculus in college would be duck soup. I was wrong. I studied long hours; I asked my roommate for help many times. Occasionally I had flashes of understanding—but they proved illusory. It never clicked. But I know better than to base my self-confidence on my understanding of calculus!

A ROLLER COASTER OF SHAME AND PRIDE

Our self-confidence grows when others trust us. The more significant the person, the more our confidence is strengthened. We feel encouraged when the boss says, "This is a very important project to our company. I've selected you to be in charge of it." Or, "I know I can count on you to do a good job on this report." A friend might tell us, "I need to talk to someone I can trust. Would you have lunch with me today?"

Yet those of us who never received a solid foundation of trust experience difficulty when it comes to healthy self-confidence. Each of the three types experience difficulties in trusting themselves. As you might expect, passive people usually avoid decisions or make them with great fear of being wrong. A deep sense of shame paralyzes them. They fear making decisions and face self-contempt if they do. Then they second-guess themselves, wishing they had made a different choice.

Aggressive people often exude arrogance, though the hard edge may be taken off by their charm. Overcompensating for their insecurities, they can't afford to be wrong or even second-best. Having to be on top, they take command through any means possible. They may be outstanding business leaders or military commanders, but tend to be poor husbands, wives, children, parents, or friends.

People who blindly trust blend these two extremes. Driven to please, they feel arrogantly indispensable when they succeed in fixing someone's problems or rallying people to a cause. But disapproval or failure quickly bursts their bubble, and they wallow in their hopelessness and shame.

Passive people exaggerate limitations and aggressive people deny them. The person who trusts blindly sees limitations in black or white, as awful like passive types or as nonexistent like aggressive types.

Some people ask, "Isn't shame just inverted pride? Both kinds of people are trusting in themselves, aren't they?" Yes, both shame and arrogance stem from the same root: insecurity and a lack of trust in God's unconditional love. But shame and pride manifest this insecurity differently. One internalizes the hopelessness and helplessness; the other overcompensates in arrogance. The root is the same, but the fruit shows a marked contrast.

Autonomy or self-confidence is the ability to make decisions, accept responsibility and consequences, and know our limitations without the excesses of self-contempt for failures or self-adulation for successes. Self-confidence is an important part of spiritual growth and health, but it must be developed with a balanced view of both weaknesses and strengths, sinfulness and spiritual gifts. Then, self-confidence becomes blended with humility instead of shame or rebellion.

CLOAKED IN SIN OR ROBED IN DIGNITY?

An accurate theological appraisal of humankind contains the dual truths of our sinfulness and the fact that we have been made in the image of God. That image has been tarnished and twisted by sin, but we nonetheless possess some degree of inherent dignity.

As with any dual truth, we generally hold tightly to one side while building a straw person on the other which justifies condemning, belittling, or dismissing the opposite end of the scale. More conservative Christians often focus on the sinfulness of humankind to the exclusion of our dignity. "The heart is desperately wicked," they remind us, but their conclusion extends to, "so don't trust your thoughts and feelings. Trust only in God and his Word."

While the ultimate source of wisdom and truth is the Bible, God acts through biblical figures and church history to give people ideas energized by their emotions. What if Moses had not perceived that God was giving him wisdom through Jethro, his father-in-law? What if the disciples had not trusted in their perceptions that Jesus was the Messiah? What if Martin Luther had not believed God was leading him to expose corruption and promote church reform? What if the great missionaries of the nineteenth century had not trusted their perceptions of God's leading and boldly taken the gospel to the world? What if millions of Christians like you and me mistrust our emotions and perceptions so much that we don't respond when God calls us to extend kindness to someone?

Those who are taught to focus on their sinfulness to the exclusion of their dignity can be easily influenced by authoritarian leaders. The message, "Don't trust in your emotions and perceptions" quickly extends to, "so you need to let me tell you what to do, what to say, and where to go." Creativity and self-expression become acceptable only within a narrow range.

Some theological persuasions claim that if we exhibit anything less than perfect love, forgiveness, peace, and joy, then something is lacking in our faith. Wanting to be "good Christians," we deny or refrain from any and all unpleasant feelings or negative perceptions. Fear and guilt drive us to redefine our lives so that we're acceptable. We're not angry; we're just "frustrated." We may be unhappy, "but still joyful." We may smile and say we love someone, even when we can't stand to look at that person. This unbalanced focus means that we can't afford to be honest about our sins.

This denial also leads us to mistrust the signals our bodies give us. The Lord "fearfully and wonderfully" made us so that we have warning lights to indicate overstressed systems. Tension headaches, stomach and other digestive tract problems, sleep disruptions, tight muscles in the neck and back, chronic fatigue, and a host of other maladies can be psychosomatic problems. Our bodies are sometimes screaming at us to slow down, get some rest, redirect priorities, find a safe environment, get help, take stock, and make changes. Ultimately, disregarding these signals may mean only that we don't function at our peak level, but we often continue to overload the system until we experience severe physical and emotional problems.

Focusing on sinfulness is good and right if we remember our dignity. But an overemphasis on sin can lead to fear and denial rather than accurate perception and healthy trust. Focusing on the opposite end can be equally destructive. Perhaps in reaction to the overemphasis on our fallen nature, some people exclusively promote the inherent honor of humankind. Others have been influenced by secular, humanistic, and deterministic teaching which describes the goodness of humanity and abhors the idea of sinfulness.

Still others have been influenced by various movements toward self-affirmation and work at seeing themselves as "perfect." "Positive thinking" taken to an extreme promotes a positive self-concept by denying personal wrongdoing. Instead of denying emotions, perceptions, and body signals, this side of the continuum tells people to live by them. We soon become self-absorbed, reflecting only on "what I think," "how I feel," and "what I want." Those who infringe on our self-fulfillment may be viewed as enemies to be avoided.

A self-centered perspective can cause trouble on various levels. Sociologically, we demand all kinds of "rights," while feeling contempt for anyone who denies them. Psychologically, this narcissism leads to a victim mentality touting "my needs above all others." Relationally, we control the behavior of others and use them to fulfill our selfish wants. Our goal is not to love but to feel happy and comfortable. Theologically, we begin to exalt experience beyond the constraints of the historical orthodox faith.

Whichever end of the continuum we find ourselves on, we often discount and condemn the perspectives of the other side. We tend to become more entrenched, less open to the ideas and arguments which can lead to equilibrium. In a healthy balance, we can admit our sinfulness without shame and self-condemnation. We experience forgiveness. We can appreciate our God-given strengths without self-preoccupation and pride. When we acknowledge that our abilities and our worth are gifts from God, we can thankfully receive them.

Recognizing our sinfulness provides humility. Recognizing our God-given abilities provides strength and courage. Believers have both human strengths and spiritual gifts (see Rom 12, 1 Cor 12, Eph 4, and 1 Pt 4) which God wants to use to advance his kingdom. As these talents, abilities, and gifts are used, we become more effective. As a loving and wise Father, God knows just how much to encourage us by using our strengths and how much to humble us by exposing our sinfulness and failures.

MARKS OF TRUE CONFIDENCE

A friend of mine who didn't react to unjust criticism was applauded for his strength of character. He secretly told me later on that he was just being passive and avoiding conflict.

This is not uncommon. Assertive leaders may be viewed as self-confident, but many use their success to earn some sense of security and approval. Rebellion and aggressive behavior sometimes look like self-confidence, but these are reactions to fear, hurt, and shame.

True self-confidence has several characteristics.

Admitting our own failures and forgiving others for theirs. Those who feel shame readily admit their own failures, but they feel victimized rather than forgiving. Those who are prideful are threatened or contemptuous of others' faults. They condemn instead of forgiving. People who have the security of trusting relationships and genuine self-confidence, however, can more readily admit their own mistakes and sins because they don't feel seriously threatened by them. They can forgive others because they've tasted forgiveness themselves.

Owning our feelings and desires. Instead of being what others want us to be or reacting against their expectations, we can be ourselves, have our own feelings, and be honest about our hopes and desires. Some of us are so crushed or enmeshed with others that we don't even know what we feel or want. Recently, I overheard several people talking about which restaurant they would go to. Somebody mentioned an Italian restaurant. As they checked with each person, one turned to her best friend and asked, "Do I like Italian?" She had to check out whether she liked a certain kind of food!

Making our own choices. "The decisions I make today are mine," a young man told me. "I hope they're right. They may be wrong. I'll seek advice from some people, but in the final analysis, I need to make my own decisions."

Accepting consequences. We're glad to accept praise for our successes, but it takes strength and security to avoid dodging the blame for our failures. "I was wrong. Please forgive me," is a message seldom heard, but it goes a long way in resolving conflict. Pointing a finger may solve the immediate problem of getting rid of the guilt, but eventually it causes more long-term strife by erecting barriers and arousing fear of more blaming.

Extending forgiveness. True self-confidence grows by failing many times and being forgiven. Failure no longer comes as a major surprise or threat. Having experienced forgiveness from others, we are better prepared to forgive those who offend us. Because forgiving someone involves acknowledging the hurt, it also involves grieving. Most of us don't want to go through the emotional turmoil of grieving our losses and forgiving the offender. It takes courage.

Being honest. Under pressure to please people—or avoid their wrath—we may be tempted to shade the truth. Confidence enables us to speak the truth, but with love and compassion. Our ultimate goal is not to blast someone, but we may have to say some hard things so that we—and others—can deal with reality instead of misperceptions. Growing maturity also teaches us that we can choose *when* we speak truth as well as *what* and *how* we speak it. Timing is very important. We need not rush in reaction to others, but we need not avoid the truth either.

Being honest applies to positive as well as negative truths. Affirmation and compliments speak the truth to people who show godly character, good work, or some other laudable trait. In fact, these attributes are even more worthy of our time and attention than the hard ones. Paul encouraged us to dwell on the positive: "Finally, brethren, whatever is true, whatever is honorable, whatever is right, whatever is pure, whatever is lovely, whatever is of good repute, if there is any excellence and if anything worthy of praise, let your mind dwell on these things" (Phil 4:8).

Using our strengths. Using the abilities and gifts God has given always involves risks. We can be puffed up by our successes or deflated by our failures. But growth and confidence enable us to skillfully use these abilities. As we do, the Lord refines both our skills and our motives. Our hearts are important to him—even more important than our abilities—and God is willing to use people who will give him honor.

We are stewards over our resources: time, money, relationships, opportunities, strengths, and spiritual gifts. Since these are gifts, we receive them and use them with thankfulness, not cockiness. Paul reminded the Corinthians, "And what do you have that you did not receive? But if you did receive it, why do you boast as if you had not received it?" (1 Cor 4:7).

Pursuing a dream. Few of us have vision; few of us dream. Today's society could be labeled bland, vanilla, and culturally numb. We especially fail to dream about how God might use us to accomplish his purposes. Perhaps the cost of commitment seems too high. Perhaps we fear the pride it would cause. As we know God better, we might expect to dream more of how we can participate in his work of building the kingdom.

Our part is to honor God by being faithful stewards; God's part is to provide the necessary wisdom and strength. But he is a patient and wise Father who doesn't always give us ease and success. God will test our resolve, purify our motives, and strengthen our faith through difficulties. As we mature through this process, our trust in God and ourselves will grow—with an appropriate mix of humility and confidence.

❖ ❖ ❖

Take Time to Reflect

1. What emotions seem out of balance in your life (either not fully developed or unstable)?

2. What does your trust orientation say about your self-esteem?

3. In what ways could you more appropriately assert your feelings?

4. What do you think forgiveness involves?

5. List several personal strengths. In what ways could you use
each one to overcome your weaknesses?

14

Whom Can You Trust?

*T*HE OTHER DAY I was looking through an old picture album and noticed a photo of a Little League baseball team. It reminded me of one of my favorite stories about my dad. My nine-year-old brother wanted to play baseball, but too many boys showed up for the city tryouts.

After all the teams had been selected, fifteen or so boys remained. The coaches and administrators huddled to figure out what to do. They knew they had to do something quickly: the boys were upset, and their parents were looking for a rope and a nearby tree! After listening for a while, my father proposed a solution. "I'll take all the rest of 'em," Dad declared. "We'll be our own team!"

Along with a friend, Dad helped them learn the game— these boys nobody else wanted. I was six years old and played an important role on the team: bat boy.

Dad followed two guiding principles in his coaching: affirm what the boys do well, and let everybody play in every game. He didn't care if it was a one-run game in the last inning, with the best hitter up next to bat with a runner on third. If a boy hadn't played yet, Dad put him in. The kids loved it! Because they knew they would get in the game, they were always excited and ready.

In the last week of the season, this group of boys nobody

wanted was tied for first place! Our team went on to win their last game (probably due to their superb bat boy!) and win the league championship! My photo commemorates a group of grinning boys celebrating a miracle season. My father had trusted in these kids—and they had trusted him—and that combination hit a home run!

Trusting others is tricky. Patterns of mistrust have led us to trust others either too much or too little. Then distorted perception reinforces our misguided trust over and over again. How can we break this vicious cycle? How can we grow in accurately appraising others so that we can make wise choices in relationships? How can we know who is worthy of our trust?

CONFUSING TRUST WITH LOVE

One of the most common misperceptions is to confuse trust with love. Many of us mistakenly believe that one requires the other. If someone trusts us, we often interpret that confidence as a signal of greater commitment than is intended, especially if we're starved for attention.

For instance, a woman who receives little emotional support at home may be competent at work. Recognizing her skills, her male supervisor gives her significant responsibility and affirmation. She may easily misinterpret his trust and affirmation, and believe his words, actions, and intentions are instead based on romantic desire. Her misinterpretation could lead to various responses: reciprocating love to her surprised supervisor; feeling angry at his inappropriate forwardness; or withdrawing because his supposed advances make her feel awkward, dirty, or guilty.

Those who trust blindly are particularly prone to confuse trusting others with loving them. They subconsciously believe their trust of another obligates that person to be kind, generous, and loving. Or they may think that trusting others magically makes them closer and sweeps away any problems in the relationship. Neither manipulation nor magic are based on reality in relationships. Trust should not be used to win love.

Trust and love, in fact, are not always related. The Scripture commands us to love others (1 Jn 4:11), even those who have wounded us (Rom 12:17-21), and to forgive the offenders (Col 3:13). We are never commanded to trust people. Scripture often commands us to seek wisdom (Prv 1:7, 10:14; Jas 1:5-8, 3:13-18). Trusting untrustworthy people isn't love; it's foolishness.

The apostle James wrote a clear explanation about the source and results of wisdom and foolishness:

Who among you is wise and understanding? Let him show by his good behavior his deeds in the gentleness of wisdom. But if you have bitter jealousy and selfish ambition in your heart, do not be arrogant and so lie against the truth. This wisdom is not that which comes down from above, but is earthly, natural, demonic. For where jealousy and selfish ambition exist, there is disorder and every evil thing. But the wisdom from above is first pure, then peaceable, gentle, reasonable, full of mercy and good fruits, unwavering, without hypocrisy. And the seed whose fruit is righteousness is sown in peace by those who make peace. James 3:13-18

Having misperceived and mistrusted others all our lives, we need God to clearly show us the consequences of our mistrust, ambitions, and defenses. We also need him to give us clear perception so that we can make wise choices. Much of this wisdom comes from being instructed by wise people. We need to talk—and especially listen—to others rich in experience and maturity. As we grow in our perceptive abilities, we will more clearly understand the contrast between wisdom and our own foolishness.

The term "foolish" may seem harsh and condemning. My intention is not to induce guilt and shame. Instead, I want to inspire convictions that will result in the clarity and strength we need to make the hard choices ahead. The following statements draw a sharp contrast between wisdom and foolishness. Perhaps you can relate to some of them, and think of many others in light of your own situation.

It is foolish to:

- Trust people who consistently wound you.
- Believe people who consistently give double messages.
- Think intimidating people have your best interests in mind.
- See people as all good or all bad.
- Withdraw from all people because some have hurt you.
- Try to figure things out by yourself.
- Seek advice from foolish people.
- Avoid conflict at all cost.
- Stir up conflict.
- Be too self-disclosing in order to earn others' love or pity.

It is wise to:

- Call on God and wise people for help.
- Be cautious about trusting people.
- Slowly elevate your level of trust in others as they prove their trustworthiness.
- Be honest with most people about your feelings and desires.
- Withhold your feelings and desires from abusive people.
- Be realistic about the growth process of learning to trust perceptively.
- Forgive and love, but not necessarily trust, others.
- Expect conflict when you are honest.
- Learn to communicate clearly and calmly with all kinds of people who mistrust.
- Realize that even trustworthy people will sometimes fail you.

TRUST IS EARNED

Those who do not earn our trust shouldn't receive it. More accurately, in the way and to the degree that people prove they can be trusted, they earn our trust. Trust can be based on someone's skills. When I try to fix our plumbing, Joyce gently reminds me of the times I've become frustrated (to put it mildly) and not done a good job. My plumbing skills don't warrant a great deal of trust.

Our perception of people's *character* usually assumes far more importance than how we see their skills. How they respond to problems and opportunities gives us an indication of their true nature. Proverbs opens many windows on our souls which help us perceive the trustworthiness of others. In response to their offenses, fools mock at sin, but the upright show good will (Prv 14:9). In their compulsive anger, fools are arrogant and careless, but the wise are cautious and turn away from evil (Prv 14:16). Fools only misuse money because they have no desire to gain wisdom (Prv 17:16).

Speech reflects a person's character. "A fool's lips bring strife, and his mouth calls for blows. A fool's mouth is his ruin, and his lips are the snare of his soul" (Prv 18:6-7). Meanwhile, the ability to listen marks a wise person. "Like an earring of gold and an ornament of fine gold is a wise reprover to a listening ear" (Prv 25:12).

How should we respond to someone who behaves like a fool? Proverbs tells us that our words, our demeanor, and the timing of our speech are all important (Prv 25:11). At times we are to be quiet (Prv 17:28), and we're always to forgive when others have hurt us (Prv 19:11). Solomon summarized the futility and pain of trying to reason with foolish people: "Let a man meet a bear robbed of her cubs, rather than a fool in his folly" (Prv 17:12).

Quite often, people want to know if they should talk to someone who has deeply hurt them. There's no easy answer to that issue. Solomon gave seemingly contradictory advice. Proverbs 26:4 says: "Do not answer a fool according to his folly, lest you also be like him." The next verse says: "Answer a fool as his folly deserves, lest he be wise in his own eyes."

How do we know when to answer and when not to answer? This passage cautions us to avoid discussion when a person is too volatile to carry on a reasonable conversation. On the other hand, sometimes we need to refute someone's foolishness, warped perception, and hurtful behavior. How do you know which kind of person is standing in front of you? If you try to reason, discuss, and resolve problems and it only gets worse, then you've got a verse-four person! You have tried, tested, and proven his or her character. This person should not be trusted.

We grow in wisdom when we learn to be perceptive of foolish behaviors. Some of us, however, refuse to trust people even when they've proven themselves worthy of our trust many times. Then the problem is not them but *us*. As we perceive the truth, we need the courage to entrust ourselves cautiously, carefully, but progressively to those who deserve it.

WEIGHING COSTS AGAINST RISKS

Sometimes we take all the right steps. We're guarded and cautious about trusting someone; we look for proof of trustworthiness; we communicate our expectations clearly. With everything as airtight as we can make it, our trust proves futile.

A few months ago we were having a book printed. We sent all the artwork to the artists. We checked their work and made changes. We double-checked the changes by fax and on the phone. We asked for the final blueline artwork, but it needed to be sent to the printer to meet a deadline. "OK," I said. "Did you make every one of the final changes I sent you?" Then I listed them once again.

"We got it." OK. It was done.

Then at the last minute, the printer goofed up several things and the book was a mess! I had been thorough, but not thorough enough to prevent the publishing-atomic-bomb goof! Even careful, cautious trust had been futile.

This incident made me think—a lot! Should I have been more demanding and tough? Maybe, but there's a risk and a cost in being so cautious that you don't trust anybody. I would rather cautiously trust people, have a relationship with them, and be disappointed occasionally, than demand such perfection in others that I crush any chance for a relationship. Instead of black or white thinking, this approach accepts the reality of risks and the cost of relating to people.

Even when we exercise proper care in trusting others we are sometimes disappointed. That's reality. Even the most trust-worthy person with the best intentions occasionally lets us down. A few months ago, I dropped Taylor off at soccer practice. I drove back home and began some paperwork. The facts and figures absorbed my attention. I was in the flow, getting the job done, making progress. Then I looked at my watch. Yikes! Soccer practice ended fifteen minutes ago. I ran out to the car and with keen powers of observation, noticed that it was raining. Hard. *How long has it been raining?* I wondered.

When I pulled into the parking lot near the soccer field, I noticed two things: one, very few cars were there (in other words, everybody else had picked up their kids long before and gone home). And two, a certain little boy looking like a wet rat glared at me as I drove up.

"I'm a bit late, huh, Son?" I said sheepishly.

"Soccer practice ended thirty minutes early because it was raining so hard." (Taylor had obviously been rehearsing that statement for a while.) "That was almost an hour ago." (I'll give my son credit. His understatement and control gave his words a flair for the dramatic.)

"So, uh... you've been out here for, uh, an hour?"

Taylor didn't say a word, but the look on his face and the water dripping off every hair, patch of skin, and fiber of clothes communicated very clearly!

"Sorry, Son."

And in typical Taylor fashion, he said cheerfully, "That's OK, Dad. What's for supper?"

I'm usually punctual, dependable, and trustworthy, but sometimes I blow it. When that happens, I'm thankful for others' forgiveness.

LEARNING THE FINE ART OF COMMUNICATION

Human relationships are not based on science; they're an art form. The foundational elements of communication and trust take on many shades of color and shapes in form and substance. Most of us find it difficult to communicate beyond the superficial. As we learn to talk about and take responsibility for our feelings, our desires, and our commitments, we can communicate them to others, opening the door for more significant relationships.

Our first efforts at discerning whom to trust inevitably produce conflict, both internal and interpersonal. When those who blindly trust become more cautious and ask more questions before they trust, and even withhold trust until individuals prove themselves, what typically happens? Accusations start to fly. "You're so selfish!" "I can't believe you would treat me this way!" "OK, I don't need you anyway!" "You don't love me anymore." These kinds of messages deeply wound—and deeply motivate—those who have trusted without question. They need strength and conviction to brave the storm and continue to grow in perceptive trust.

Passive individuals are afraid that honest communication of feelings and desires will reveal what they fear most: that people really don't care. When they assert themselves, even carefully, they run the risk of hearing someone snap, "Who asked you, anyway?" "So the church mouse has an opinion, huh? Well, what do you know?" "Aw, you don't know anything! You never have!" These kinds of statements—usually accompanied by a condemning tone of voice and facial gestures—threaten to drive passive people back into their holes. They need confidence and clarity to continue their efforts at asserting themselves.

Aggressive people need a special kind of courage: the strength to be weak and not overpowering. Instead of having all the answers and being the center of attention, the aggressive person needs to ask, "Would you tell me how I affect you? I want to change. Please help me by being honest." Then they need to listen, without explaining or defending. Just listen. Others will probably be surprised and quite hesitant about being so open and honest. Those who have a track record of aggressive distrust must courageously continue to pursue this openness which they find so threatening.

When we begin to communicate more clearly and honestly with others, we will learn a lot about ourselves and about them. We will probably gain insight into their true natures. Though people's initial response may be quite defensive, they may be far more open than we imagined if we give them time to reflect.

Our honest communication may be the catalyst for change in the lives of others. Sometimes people harden, but sometimes they repent. "I know I've let you down," one man told his wife. "But I see I've hurt you and the children so much. I want to change. What can I do?" Such statements may be only attempts to buy time and divert the problem. But sometimes the repentance proves genuine. These individuals need our continued support and clear, honest communication. But we still need to be sure they prove themselves by taking specific actions and really change.

Sometimes our honesty confirms our darkest suspicions. In talking through difficulties, some people harden. They blame us for everything; their venom intensifies. Although disappointing, this revelation helps us tremendously. No longer must we live in the blind hope that "they really don't mean what they say." These people should not be trusted.

What if someone says all the right things but breaks one promise after another? How long should we keep forgiving and communicating before we decide that person isn't trustworthy? Each of us must answer that question in light of the particular relationship. Even though God calls us to keep extending forgiveness, a person's continued unwillingness to resolve problems after repeated attempts may finally convince us to relinquish hope.

DO TRUST AND FORGIVENESS GO HAND IN HAND?

Just as trust does not necessarily follow in the footsteps of love, trust doesn't necessarily result from forgiveness. But many of us believe if we forgive someone, we must then trust him or her. This belief leads to two potential problems: forgiving and feeling obligated to trust untrustworthy people; or refusing to forgive because we refuse to trust the other person.

Forgiveness, however, is unilateral. It can be extended without any requirement that we trust or any demand that the other person become trustworthy. If we can extricate the concept of forgiveness from the quagmire of untrustworthy relationships, we can both experience and express forgiveness with no strings attached.

A friend of mine was deeply hurt by her husband. As the children grew, he seemed more and more out of control. He was uptight around them, and sometimes his smoldering volcano of anger erupted. This man's anger also often landed on his wife as well. He criticized her clothes, her work, her friends, virtually every aspect of her life. The months and years of oppressive, constant fault-finding had taken their toll on the relationship. My friend felt bitter and hurt, and she often responded by criticizing her husband.

I talked with her about forgiveness. "I can't forgive him!" she blurted out. I understood her deep resentment, but she went on to add a twist. "If I *forgive* him, I'll have to *trust* him. And I don't ever want to get close to him, let him know anything about me, or tell him how I feel again."

"But the Lord doesn't ask you to *trust* him," I told her, "just to *forgive* him."

This woman looked puzzled. We talked at length about how foolish it would be to trust someone who continues to be untrustworthy.

"I hope he will begin to change as you work through the hurt and anger together, but he may not. As much as he changes, as much as he proves to be trustworthy, you can wisely trust him. Not more, and not less."

Those who trust blindly and those who passively distrust tend to excuse the offender and blame themselves for bruises and breaks in relationships. They may say, "I forgive," but they really only excuse or minimize the wound. Once their guilt-tank fills up, they blame anyone and everyone for even the slightest offense. Meanwhile they continue to trust someone who is not trustworthy.

Their aggressive counterparts begin (and end) by excusing themselves and blaming others for relationship problems. Forgiveness comes to mean acknowledging that the other person was wrong, and then trying to live with it. Just as none of these types trust wisely, none of them forgives well, which leads to relationships increasingly marred by bitterness, hurt, withdrawal, and attack.

RESTORING TRUST

In order to put an embittering event behind us, some people encourage us to "forgive and forget," but that may not be the whole story. We cannot nor should not expect amnesia as a response to injury. The Scriptures teach us to go to the person who has hurt us (Mt 18:15; Gal 6:1) and speak boldly and clearly to the offender. We should aim toward resolution and reconciliation, not vengeance. If all goes well, our communication will clarify the issues, bring about forgiveness, and begin the process of restoration.

In *Unfinished Business,* Charles Sell comments on the benefits—and even the necessity—of this vital step:

> Confrontation is one of the best ways to let go of bitterness. Too often people hold on to resentment because the wrong has never been dealt with. When someone sins, is rebuked, and truly repents, truth is declared. If we secretly, silently try to forgive people who have grossly wronged us, we get more confused about right and wrong. We have a need to distinguish between normal and abnormal, just and unjust. To simply write off wrong actions brutalizes our sense of justice.[1]

When we forgive someone, we don't have to trust them. But extending forgiveness at least begins the restoration of trust in the relationship. It clears away the barrier of bitterness—at least on our side—so that we can be open to the possibility of healing and growth between ourselves and the person involved. We can choose to love and return good for evil, while being careful not to expose ourselves to those who still refuse to take appropriate steps to change—thereby proving their untrustworthiness.

"I've forgiven her and offered to rebuild our relationship," a man told me about his wife. "I hope she responds to my invitation to make slow, steady progress. I'm through with the drastic pendulum swings of blind trust, then reacting to hurt by not trusting at all. Now I want to see real communication, real resolution, and a real relationship instead of all the games we've played."

Forgiveness started the process, and forgiveness of new hurts continues to keep the door open, but trust is built slowly, brick by brick. We can forgive others whether they ask for it or not, whether they will offend us again or not, whether they did it deliberately or not, and whether we feel like it or not. Without forgiving those who have hurt us, we will not be able to wisely decide if they are worthy of our trust.

People of all types can feel justified in their mistrust and mis-perception. It makes sense to them. Mistrust has worked—to some degree at least. Though it has allowed some pain, these individuals still find mistrust much more comfortable than fac-ing reality. Even the thought of change is threatening; actually doing it requires real courage.

As we said earlier, trusting others cannot be reduced to a formula. But perceptive trust imparts the wisdom and courage we need to build strong relationships with trustworthy people, even while we continue to be cautious with everyone.

❖ ❖ ❖

Take Time to Reflect

1. In what ways have you inadvertently allowed relationships to fail because you trusted too much? Not enough?

2. In your experience, what personal qualities suggest a person is trustworthy? Untrustworthy?

3. What do you find yourself focusing upon when you're lis-tening to another person?

4. How well do you listen to yourself? Explain. What ways can you show others you trust them?

5. In your communication with others, how can you show that you've listened?

15

Becoming Worthy of Trust

WHEN I WAS ABOUT TWELVE YEARS OLD, several elderly ladies observed one of my behavioral patterns which more or less killed my credibility. My grandmother lived with us after my grandfather died. Every Wednesday afternoon, she and three friends played bridge at one of their houses.

These ladies were a riot! They played for blood. My grandmother stewed about her partner's bad play that lost the game. "She should have bid three hearts and played the high trumps on Eliza's spade run. I can't believe she didn't see it!" Wars have been started over less! All the ladies had their own superstitions, but Mrs. Eliza Morgan's won the prize. She always put a napkin on her head for good luck. Quite a sight.

I was your run-of-the-mill boy. I liked sports and camping and hot dogs and snakes, not necessarily in that order. In fact, I kept a few choice snakes caged in the basement. Over the course of my herpetology career, I had a Florida king snake, an Eastern hognose, a five-foot racer, and a couple of six-foot blacksnakes. The cage I built was just fine for a two-foot hognose, but these huge blacksnakes were something else!

One fateful Wednesday after school, I came in the front door, greeted the ladies playing bridge, and headed to the basement to check on my blacksnakes. I looked in the cage and found nothing! I searched all over the basement for those two monsters, but couldn't find them. No problem. They would turn up somewhere.

I walked upstairs and into the room where the bridge game was being played. With a completely calm voice, I said, "Grandmamma, my snakes have gotten out of the cage. If you see them, would you let me know?"

Before my eyes, four little old ladies turned into decathlon champions. They threw their cards on the table, jumped up, grabbed their coats, and bolted for the door! They muttered a few words amid all the commotion, but I couldn't make them out. Probably just as well.

I believe in the sovereignty of God, but I'm not sure those ladies did. They refused to play bridge at our house for months. Finally, my grandmother convinced her friends that the snakes were gone and the house was completely safe. The bridge club could resume in safety.

On another Wednesday afternoon during the winter, I decided to work on my Boy Scout merit badge for firemanship. After a quick snack, I headed down to the field behind the house. A deep ravine ran down the middle of it, and the whole three-acre field was covered with the skeletons of dead kudzu plants. (For those of you who aren't from the South, kudzu is "the vine that ate Atlanta." Some person without much foresight introduced it in the thirties to stop soil erosion. Kudzu grows at an almost observable rate—several inches a day—but in the winter, all the leaves die and the thick web of vines dries up and becomes brittle—and flammable.)

I built a small fire in the bottom of the ravine, successfully put it out, built another one, and put it out, too. This procedure wasn't actually required for the merit badge, but I wanted to try some creative approaches. After the tenth or twelfth fire, a strong gust of wind suddenly swept down the ravine and carried the little fire into the tangled mass of kudzu vines. The dry vines quickly ignited and spread up the ravine walls. I tried to stomp out the flames, but they were spreading too fast. Beating them out with a stick didn't work either.

In only a few seconds, the flames had spread for twenty feet in all directions. What could I do? I ran back to the house, through the basement door, and called the fire department. I kept watching the billowing gray smoke as the fire spread quickly in the wind. I realized the fire would reach a nearby fence in a minute or two, and just past the fence sat one of the biggest houses in town. With no time to waste, I started running up the basement stairs. Near the top of the stairs, I slowed down. I didn't want to frighten the ladies in the bridge club. (I remembered the snakes; they probably did too.)

I walked calmly to the table and said matter-of-factly, "Grandmamma, when the fire truck comes, tell them to come around to the back of the house."

Déjà vu. The geriatric decathletes sprung into action again! They were out the door in a flash! This time I understood a few more words they muttered. They didn't seem appreciative of how considerate I had been in staying calm.

This time it was even longer before the bridge club met again at our house. I think they wanted some written assurance that I would be away at camp or somewhere out of the country. They sensed a pattern in my behavior, and they didn't trust me. (If you ask me, anybody who puts a napkin on her head doesn't have much room to question anybody else's trustworthiness!)

As we grow in our ability to perceive and communicate, we ourselves become more trustworthy. Perhaps you feel offended by the implication that you are less than trustworthy now, but doesn't pleasing people at all costs show a lack of personal integrity? Isn't hiding from others also hiding from our responsibility to be honest with them? Doesn't our use of intimidation make us less than safe?

Our aim is to trust wisely, to react appropriately, to communicate honestly, to give and receive love more freely. We learn not to make commitments we aren't willing to keep, and then to follow through. Such traits make us safer, more worthy of trust. Some people will be offended or angered by a closer encounter with truth. Others, however, will recognize the safety we now offer by our growing faithfulness, consistency, and integrity. They will see us forgiving and listening, being strong and kind.

Our goal, then, is not only finding the right people to trust, but also being the right people to be trusted. Several important elements blend and converge to build character and trustworthiness. The steps we take to identify and resolve these issues work at a very deep level in our lives. Through that process, we become safer and more dependable people.

A SENSE OF ENTITLEMENT

Unfortunately, many of us become sidetracked along the way. As we discussed in chapter ten, a sense of entitlement—or demandingness—can keep us stuck in bitterness. We've been hurt. Others haven't been trustworthy. They've let us down. We expect and demand that the scales be balanced: people have made us unhappy; now they must make us happy, healthy, and well. It's only fair. When others don't treat us perfectly, we pout, sulk, withdraw, or attack.

These responses certainly don't make us safe and loving. We become just the opposite of what we want others to be for us! This victim mentality dumps us squarely into a mud puddle of self-pity, expecting a knight to ride up on a white horse and make us happy. Then when the knight arrives with tarnished armor and a dirty horse, we blame him for not caring. We look for another... and another... and....

We lose all perspective. We want it all—now! We see the glass as half-empty instead of half-full. We may be blindly trusting others to fix us, or hopeless that anyone will ever make us happy. Or we may feel driven to get what we deserve no matter what the cost. Or both.

"I've always had a sort of helpless-demanding attitude,"

Cathy reflected. "I didn't realize it was wrong. I didn't realize where it came from, but it was a real plague! I went from relationship to relationship—two husbands, lots of friends, people at church—looking for someone to make me happy. When they felt sorry for me, I'd feel stronger. When they got tired of me and dumped me, I was furious. Oh, don't get me wrong, I wasn't a wallflower. I was very active in church and at work, but I was passive in relationships. Only a year ago, I began realizing this pattern. It seems pretty stupid to live it so long and not see it!"

A sense of entitlement is a product of our mistrust, and it perpetuates our mistrust. When we look through these distorted lenses and see people meeting our needs, we feel justified. When they don't, our demands intensify. The painful cycle continues. Demandingness soon squeezes out contentment, thankfulness, and love.

Rather than being black or white, life is colored in countless shades of gray. Gray issues require more wisdom and discernment and resolve. Recognizing that life is gray means accepting reality; sometimes life is disappointing (but we don't need to go into a tailspin) and we *can* find both love and joy (without idealizing).

God wants us to learn how to blend dependence on him and decision-making wisdom: faith and discernment. We gradually come to appreciate divine grace at work. He puts us into circumstances to develop our wisdom and trust in him. Wise perception views these events as a school for our growth instead of threats. Rather than helping us to escape difficulties, God wants to teach us how to trust him right in the thick of trouble.

In his wisdom, God often links us with difficult people to make us more trustworthy. He may allow a woman who blindly trusts to be in a relationship with an abrasive person who doesn't appreciate her. He may allow a passive man to relate to a critical person who continues to pursue the relationship even though he's been given lots of signals to go away. God may bring aggressive people together with someone who is willing to confront them. Or they may find themselves around someone who is a little smarter, a little more effective, and a little more successful.

Should we choose to stay and take the heat? Not always. Sometimes we need the strength to leave, sometimes the strength to stay and resolve conflict after conflict, and sometimes we need the strength to listen without defending ourselves.

I certainly don't mean to condone or minimize another person's wrongdoing or abusive behavior. But with all of our probing into past wounds, we sometimes need to simply focus on current situations and relationships. In the unfathomable sovereignty and permissive will of God, he allows sinful people to hurt others. Having been victimized in the past doesn't mean we have to remain victims today, or that we need to victimize others. We can see life differently now through new lenses, with new hope and new wisdom.

Whether our traumas have been self-inflicted, the consequence of someone else's wrongdoing, or by the sovereign hand of God, they can all result in greater dependence on God. He wants to use our difficulties to help us grow in faith, wisdom, and discernment. In the process we understand the struggles of others because we have experienced our own. We realize how hard it is to be faithful because we have experienced temptation.

Our growing compassion is not lost on others. They can sense a new strength, coupled with gentleness and quickness to forgive. They learn to see us as approachable because we don't condemn them or try to fix them. And they find us more dependable because we can share with them the wisdom we are learning. We are becoming more worthy of trust.

STRENGTH IN WEAKNESS

Having felt threatened in the past, we may have been afraid to admit we were wrong. Or perhaps we soaked up faults like a blame sponge to avoid honestly confronting others with their hurtful behavior. As we grow in wisdom and trust, we can more readily acknowledge our fallenness and our need for repentance. And because we know some of the folly caused by our own wayward choices, we recognize our need for God to direct us.

Strangely, admitting our weaknesses imparts courage and strength. As we invite God's Spirit to work in us, our confidence grows. We echo Paul's paradoxical statement, "When I am weak, then I am strong" (2 Cor 12:10). We may not be right all the time, but who wants to be around a know-it-all? We may not avoid conflict at all costs anymore, but now others realize they can relate to us as people instead of fragile china dolls. We may not be top dog all the time, but we slowly realize that love is more valuable than power.

Because of our mistrust, many of us have been unapproachable. Our anger, criticisms, defiance, and quick answers have sent out a clear signal: "Stay away. I'm not safe." Many of us have coupled that message with an added threat: "You'd better do exactly as I say... or else!" We may even throw in a third: "I really appreciate you because you did that for me!" We feel oppressed and trapped by these messages; others do, too. We need to consider if we communicate those messages to others and how they reveal that we aren't safe or dependable.

Some of us face the opposite problem. We are *too* approachable—like a doormat. We may leave a room to avoid painful, honest contact with someone. We may change the subject to something more pleasant so we won't have to face reality. We may consistently avoid risks, relationships, and new experiences. These actions violate cardinal tenants of trust: honesty and integrity. We aren't safe or dependable if we refuse to wade into a relationship and resolve problems. We may need help to work through thornier issues. And the problem may never be resolved. But the willingness to hang in there and keep going turns out to be a fundamental characteristic of a trustworthy person.

We are learning that safe people let us make our own choices and experience the consequences. We need to reciprocate and not control others—whether they try to control us or not. We may have to set limits on unacceptable behavior, but we let people make their own choices.

Our willingness to value people's freedom to choose strikes me as very rare, even in the church. Genuine love does not manipulate. This kind of love can speak volumes to unbelievers. Visitors notice such things and are attracted or repulsed by what they see. As one of the distinguishing ingredients in Christian love, the absence of manipulation can aid our evangelistic efforts (see Jn 13:34-35).

Charles Swindoll describes the positive impact of love without manipulation in his book *The Grace Awakening*. "Be an accepting model of grace. Refuse all temptations to be a brother basher or sister smasher. We already have too many of them roaming around the religious landscape. And nothing catches the attention of the unsaved world quicker than those times when we Christians beat up on one another. Don't think the unsaved world doesn't notice our cannibalism."[1]

MOLDED BY GRACE

The more we understand the trustworthiness of God, the more secure and worthy of trust we ourselves become. Our character is changed. The powerful become meek, and the helpless grow in strength. The smart learn to listen, and the ignorant become wise.

Experiencing more of God's grace opens the door to healthy relationships: we can love others as God loves us (1 Jn 4:10-11); we can accept others in the same way that he accepts us (Rom 15:7); and we can forgive others because we are overwhelmed with the fact that God has forgiven us (Eph 4:32). Learning how to express these elements of divine grace may be slow, but trustworthiness is a strength that is forged over time.

Becoming trustworthy is much like learning to trust. You

need to be prepared for each choice, each event, each encounter. Think through your normal reactions, and decide in advance how you want to respond the next time around. Write it down and keep it with you in case you need some direction and encouragement. And seek help. Ask a trusted friend to tell you in which ways you are trustworthy and in which ways you aren't. As you grow stronger or if the situation warrants (especially for aggressive people), ask the important people in your life the same question. Then listen.

I have personally watched many people grow tremendously in wisdom and perceptive trust. Joan who has always tended to trust blindly, to say the right thing, and to do the right thing to win approval, is learning to have her own opinions. She can disagree with others without demanding they change their views to fit her own. Joan used to gravitate toward those who were either pitiful and needed her, or powerful and dominated her. Now she sees the pathology of both attractions. Her growing stability, autonomy, and identity give her more wisdom in relationships. "I actually have friends now who don't desperately need me!" she laughs.

Sherry, who has been quite passive, is growing in authentic strength. "I used to get so confused when I was in any kind of strained conversation," she told me. "It was like being paralyzed. But over the past couple of years, I'm learning to have clearer goals in relationships, even in conversations. At first, I had to write down every word and read it to the person I needed to be honest with." Sherry smiled, remembering the beginning of her progress. "Now, I still like to write to clarify my thinking, but I can more clearly say what I want to without being paralyzed or exploding."

Larry used to be tough as nails and mean as a snake—an apt description of aggressive distrust. Like most aggressive people, he had to go through devastating experiences in order to see his need. Larry had always handled pressures easily. In fact, he had created most of them so he could be the hero when he solved them. But the pressures suddenly became too great.

This man's marriage began to falter. His teenage son left home. His business took a nose dive. This time, his old style of controlling others through intimidation made each situation worse.

In one of the most difficult moments of his life, Larry called a trusted friend and asked to meet with him. Over the next several months, the two met and talked. This friend spoke the truth and was not intimidated by Larry's bluffs and excuses. The hard exterior began to crack, and the tears of hurt and fear and sorrow came.

Today Larry can still be tough as nails and mean as a snake, but he usually catches himself and apologizes. His work style still reflects his sharp mind and rapid pace and hard-charging drive, but the level of intensity has toned way down. Now this man listens to people who interrupt with a question. Previously aloof, distant, and demanding, Larry is far more approachable for his wife, his son, his employees, and God.

The changes in these people's lives are dramatic, but the transition is not yet complete. They continue to carry traits of their mistrust, but these characteristics can now be strengths instead of weaknesses. Joan still has the ability to read everyone's slightest mood change, but now she isn't compelled to act on this perception by pleasing others no matter what. Sherry is still cautious but no longer paralyzed. She asks a second or third question to be sure of a person or a situation, and then makes decisions based on answers to those questions. Larry still gets a lot done, but now he values people in the process instead of using them.

Change is possible.

DOES GOD TRUST US?

As our Bible study group discussed this issue of being trusted by others, someone asked, "Does God trust us?"

I found that an intriguing concept. I think my answer is, "Not exactly." Trust implies that the one doing the trusting needs something from the one being trusted. God is self-existent; he has no needs at all. Even so, he has chosen to have a relationship with us, which includes entrusting certain things to us as his stewards. For example, he entrusted the Old Testament law and the oracles to the Jewish people, expecting them to value, guard, and teach his truth to all nations (Rom 3:2). And God specifically entrusted the Ten Commandments to Moses (Acts 7:38).

God has now entrusted the ministry of the gospel to all believers who have been reconciled by Christ's payment for our sins and given new life through the resurrection. Scripture calls us "ambassadors for Christ," which suggests that God is entreating the world through us (2 Cor 5:19-20).

Perhaps the most astounding aspect of our stewardship is found in Jesus' prayer shortly before his death: God has entrusted his glory to us (Jn 17:22-23). We are the caretakers of his reputation and his character among humankind. Jesus specifically says in this passage that our relationship with other believers can bring glory to God. In other words, what we say and do toward one another reflects on what others think of him. What an incredible privilege, and an awesome responsibility.

Finally, Paul links the concept of stewardship with our familial relationship with God. As his children, we inherit his riches and responsibilities. We share with him in the good and the bad, just as a family shares those times together. In our case, Paul refers to the difficulties we experience and the promise of God's nearness and strength: "And if children, heirs also, heirs of God and fellow heirs with Christ, if indeed we suffer with him in order that we may also be glorified with him" (Rom 8:17).

God has entrusted to us a great deal. He knows that we can do all things by his grace, so perhaps he's trusting in us to trust in him. Yet God knows our fears well. Otherwise, he wouldn't assure us so often of his purposes and his presence. We feel hurt and alone; God says he cares. We feel angry and resentful; God promises wisdom and strength. We feel ashamed; God grants forgiveness and comfort.

In his letter to the Roman Christians, Paul recounts a litany of the effects of God's goodness toward us: we are forgiven;

strengthened by his Spirit; granted wisdom, sonship, and hope. We are promised the prayers of Christ for our needs and the certainty of an eternal destiny and purpose. Paul then asks: "What then shall we say to these things? If God is for us, who is against us? He who did not spare his own Son, but delivered him up for us all, how will he not also with him freely give us all things?" (Rom 8:31-32).

We continually experience hardships. People disappoint us. We disappoint ourselves. But God is constant and compassionate. We are not alone. He cares. Against all reason, the transcendent God loves us so much that he has committed himself to us. That is why Paul could proclaim: "But in all these things we overwhelmingly conquer through him who loved us. For I am convinced that neither death, nor life, nor angels, nor principalities, nor things present, nor things to come, nor powers, nor height, nor depth, nor any other created thing, shall be able to separate us from the love of God, which is in Christ Jesus our Lord" (Rom 8:37-39).

Our God is uniquely and ultimately trustworthy. May we find our peace, rest, hope, and joy in him.

❖ ❖ ❖

Take Time to Reflect

1. In what ways are you trustworthy?

2. In what ways are you less than trustworthy?

3. What concrete steps can you take to become a safer, more dependable person?

4. Do you have a sense of hope that the Lord is for you? Why or why not?

Using *Trusting* in Groups

TRUSTING is designed to be used both individually and in groups. In fact, individual reading and reflection combined with group interaction is most helpful.

The book can be used as a supplement to support group material. If the facilitator realizes that the group members are resistant and having difficulty making progress, he or she may use *Trusting* for a few weeks to stimulate reflection, discussion, and steps forward.

In the context of an ongoing support group, you may want to have the group focus on a few particular chapters in the book, or you can study the entire book as a thirteen-week hiatus from the usual material.

Quarterly growth groups can also effectively use *Trusting*. Many churches use these groups to get people more in touch with relational, emotional, and spiritual hurts and needs. After a few quarters, many groups seem to "bog down." Some people may be ready and willing to make real progress, but others are hesitant. *Trusting* can be useful in helping the group members to understand their hesitancy and give them wisdom and courage to keep going in their recovery process.

The questions at the end of each chapter will aid reflection and discussion. The best method, obviously, is for group members to read and answer the questions before they come to the group. Then, discussion will be more meaningful.

In either support groups or growth groups, we recommend the following thirteen-week format:

Week 1 ....Chapters 1 and 2

Week 2 ....Chapters 3 and 4

Week 3 ....Chapter 5

Week 4 ....Chapter 6

Week 5 ....Chapter 7

Week 6 ....Chapter 8

Week 7 ....Chapter 9

Week 8 ....Chapter 10

Week 9 ....Chapter 11

Week 10 ....Chapter 12

Week 11 ....Chapter 13

Week 12 ....Chapter 14

Week 13 ....Chapter 15

Author's Note

Perhaps reading this book has raised your awareness of deep hurts and strained relationships in your life—or in the life of someone you love.

Many people want help, but they do not know where to turn. They want to talk to someone who understands their problems and who will give them answers which are consistent with their Christian faith. I am a consultant for Rapha Treatment Centers. I recommend that you call them for help.

Rapha is one of the nation's largest managers of psychiatric care and substance abuse treatment from a distinctively Christian perspective. Rapha offers a continuum of care for adults and adolescents including acute inpatient, sub-acute, and partial hospitalization; day, evening, and weekend programs; intensive outpatient services; an outpatient network; conferences; support group training; books and other materials. To talk to a confidential inquiry counselor, call 1-800-383-4673.

—Pat Springle

Notes

TWO
Retracing Your Steps

1. Eugene McDonald, "Emotional Growth of the Child," *Texas Medicine*, 63 (1967), 73-79.
2. Dr. Theodore Lidz of the Yale School of Medicine, *The Person* (New York, N.Y.: Basic Books, 1968), 117.
3. Les Parrot III, *Helping the Struggling Adolescent* (Grand Rapids, MI: Zondervan, 1992), 163.

THREE
The Shattering of Trust

1. T.S. Holmes and R.H. Rahe, "The Social Readjustment Scale," *Journal of Psychosomatic Research*, Vol. II (1967), 213-18, as cited in *Psychological Testing: Principles, Applications and Issues* (Pacific Grove, CA: Brook/ Cole, 1972), 445-8.

EIGHT
Charm and Venom

1. Dan Allender, *The Wounded Heart* (Colorado Springs, CO: NavPress, 1990), 162-63.
2. Charles Colson, J.I. Packer, R.C. Sproul, Alister McGrath, and others, *Power Religion* (Chicago, IL: Moody, 1992), 28.

ELEVEN
Learning to Trust Perceptively

1. There are many resources that can help you confront others more wisely and effectively, including *Caring Enough to Confront* by David Augs-

burger, *Forgive and Forget* by Lewis Smedes, and *The Wounded Heart* by Dan Allender.

TWELVE
Hobbled by Unbelief

1. J.I. Packer, *Knowing God* (Downers Grove, IL: InterVarsity Press with permission from Hodder and Stoughton Limited, London), 226-27.
2. Jerry Bridges, *Trusting God* (Colorado Springs, CO: NavPress, 1990), 57-58.
3. B.F. Wescott, *The Epistle to the Hebrews, Second Edition* (London: Macmillan, 1892), 127, as cited in W. Bingham Hunter, *The God Who Hears* (Downers Grove, IL: InterVarsity Press, 1986), 159.

FOURTEEN
Whom Can You Trust?

1. Charles Sell, *Unfinished Business* (Portland, OR: Multnomah, 1989), 137.

FIFTEEN
Becoming Worthy of Trust

1. Charles R. Swindoll, *The Grace Awakening* (Dallas, TX: Word, 1990), 163.